PRAISE FOR *THE THEFT OF AMERICA'S SOUL*

"The moral clarity in this book is so powerful and so refreshing I wish I could give it to everyone I know. Incidentally, the only way something could be this full of truth and wisdom is if its author is a prophet. That he is. Hear him."

—ERIC METAXAS, AUTHOR OF *BONHOEFFER* AND *IF YOU CAN KEEP IT*

"In *The Theft of America's Soul*, the Duck Commander has set his sights on something higher, taking aim at the ten lies that have led our culture astray and put our faith, our families, and our freedom at risk. I am grateful for the direct, nonpolitically correct way my friend Phil Robertson lays out the truth. My prayer is that this book finds its way into the hands and hearts of many Americans."

—TONY PERKINS, PRESIDENT OF FAMILY RESEARCH COUNCIL AND PRESIDENT OF COUNCIL FOR NATIONAL POLICY

"During these days and in this world, we need a direct, clear, and positively disruptive message about what the Bible says about living life the right way. Phil Robertson's voice is unique in that he not only speaks the truth, but he has been living these truths as a matter of faith and integrity for many years. His authenticity and his challenges will speak to you."

—DR. JOHN TOWNSEND, *NEW YORK TIMES* BESTSELLING AUTHOR AND FOUNDER OF THE TOWNSEND INSTITUTE OF LEADERSHIP AND COUNSELING

"Phil Robertson is not only my friend, he's someone I admire for his boldness when it comes to the truth of God's word and his ability to shoot straight. He is known by millions of people who have watched him on television and marveled at the family he and his wife, Miss Kay, have raised to love God, family, and country. Phil is a man who doesn't beat around the bush. He doesn't sugarcoat what is going on in our world today and once again sounds the alarm as he lays out the case for *The Theft of America's Soul*."

—FRANKLIN GRAHAM, PRESIDENT AND CEO OF SAMARITAN'S PURSE, BILLY GRAHAM EVANGELISTIC ASSOCIATION

"Something I know for sure is that Phil Robertson loves God, his family, people, and our country. In *The Theft of America's Soul* he candidly shares new and personal stories while powerfully and compellingly presenting spiritual solutions to our current culture war."

—ROBERT MORRIS, LEAD SENIOR PASTOR OF GATEWAY
CHURCH AND BESTSELLING AUTHOR OF *THE BLESSED*
LIFE, *THE GOD I NEVER KNEW*, AND *FREQUENCY*

"America is in desperate need of a cultural awakening that would restore God to the public square. Phil Robertson has done a masterful job of diagnosing the central problem, the lies that have their roots in the Father of Lies. Those lies are acted on by Christians as well as unbelievers, to the harm of every part of our country. *The Theft of America's Soul* exposes the ten primary lies the devil has used in an attempt to steal, kill, and destroy America's soul. Phil provides ten truths from the Bible that, if believed and acted on, would put God back into the culture and might just turn our country around. This is a must-read for every Christian."

—DR. ROBERT JEFFRESS, SENIOR PASTOR AT
FIRST BAPTIST CHURCH, DALLAS

"It seems across America that 'truth has fallen in the streets.' Phil Robertson has rejected political correctness and speaks to us with common sense and faith. Put this book on your must-read list."

—PASTOR ALLEN JACKSON, PASTOR OF WORLD OUTREACH
CHURCH, MURFREESBORO, TENNESSEE

THE THEFT OF
AMERICA'S SOUL

THE THEFT OF AMERICA'S SOUL

BLOWING THE LID OFF THE LIES THAT ARE DESTROYING OUR COUNTRY

PHIL ROBERTSON

WITH SETH HAINES

NELSON
BOOKS

An Imprint of Thomas Nelson

Published in Nashville, Tennessee, by Nelson Books, an imprint of Thomas Nelson. Nelson Books and Thomas Nelson are registered trademarks of HarperCollins Christian Publishing, Inc.

Published in association with Yates & Yates, www.yates2.com.

Thomas Nelson titles may be purchased in bulk for educational, business, fundraising, or sales promotional use. For information, please email SpecialMarkets@ ThomasNelson.com.

Unless otherwise noted, Scripture quotations are taken from the Holy Bible, New International Version®, niv®. Copyright © 1973, 1978, 1984, 2011 by Biblica, Inc.® Used by permission of Zondervan. All rights reserved worldwide. www.Zondervan. com. The "niv" and "New International Version" are trademarks registered in the United States Patent and Trademark Office by Biblica, Inc.®

Scripture quotations marked nkjv are from the New King James Version®. © 1982 by Thomas Nelson. Used by permission. All rights reserved.

Scripture quotations marked rsv are from Revised Standard Version of the Bible. Copyright 1946, 1952, and 1971 National Council of the Churches of Christ in the United States of America. Used by permission. All rights reserved.

ISBN 978-1-4002-1004-6 (HC)
ISBN 978-1-4002-1005-3 (eBook)

Library of Congress Cataloging-in-Publication Data

Library of Congress Control Number: 2018957875

Printed in the United States of America

19 20 21 22 23   LSC   10 9 8 7 6 5 4 3 2 1

This book is dedicated to the only One who can give inalienable rights, the One who provides absolute truth to shape cultures, the One to whom every knee shall bow: Almighty God, the Creator and Father of us all.

CONTENTS

INTRODUCTION

I n April 1966 *Time* raised a ruckus when it printed this question in red block letters against a black background on its cover: "Is God Dead?"

It was a shocking cover posing a shocking question, and that question took root in the public dialogue of the day. Scientists, preachers, insurance agents, housewives—everyone from New York to California was drawn into the discussion. Even us river rats down in Northern Louisiana. But if the cover was provocative, the story inside the magazine was even more provocative.

"Is God dead?" the article opened. "It is a question that tantalizes both believers, who perhaps secretly fear that he is, and atheists, who possibly suspect that the answer is no." The writer added that modern churchmen were trying to reconcile God's supposed death with their brand of Christianity. "A small band of radical theologians," he wrote, "has seriously argued that the chorus must accept the fact of God's death, and get along without him." These theologians believed it was time for the church to figure out a way to "write a theology without theos, without God."[1]

Huh?

The disappearance of God in art, politics, and economics led to the death of God, some claimed in the article. Modern science had undermined or explained the mysteries of God in the natural world, others said. And in the wake of God's supposed death, many believers in the modern church turned to other things in search of meaning. Psychiatry, Zen, and drugs were the new sources of meaning for so many. Others had "quietly abandoned all but token allegiance to the churches, surrendering themselves to a life of 'anonymous Christianity' dedicated to civil rights or the Peace Corps."

Anonymous Christianity.

What in the world?

This *Time* article explored the very things I'd hear on my college campus at Louisiana Tech University later that year. My professors hung their hats on Nietzsche, Darwin, and Freud. Man's ancestors crawled out of the salt water, they said. Man's notions of right and wrong were taught, handed down; morality was a set of fabricated human constructs, they said. Morality was relative. Sexuality was relative. Nothing was absolute. God, the old white-bearded judge in the sky, was a myth. What's more, professor after professor implied that if man could liberate himself from this archaic myth, he'd find true freedom.

Man could be his own judge.

Man could be his own master.

Man could be the arbiter of his own freedom.

Man could be the center of his own existence.

Today many point to that *Time* article as the first time the elephant in the room—the question of whether God was still hanging around—was addressed in the broader market. Some of those same folks point to that article as the culmination of 1960s enlightenment. I know the truth about the sixties, because I lived them. The truth is, the sixties were anything but enlightened. They were very dark.

In the sixties a deep sleep–ism settled over our country. Atheism, agnosticism, humanism, moral relativism, naturalism, personalism, rationalism, materialism—all the isms washed over us. These isms led America deeper into sexual immorality, greed, and the wholesale slaughter of the unborn. The isms led us into debauchery. I know this because, to my embarrassment, those isms washed over me. For a time they led me down the same road of sin, a road I'll write more about later in this book.

It's been more than fifty years since the publication of that *Time* article, and almost as many years since I was freed from the lies written about in that article. How was I freed? Only through an encounter with the living God.

The last time I checked, God ain't dead. He is very much alive. It's a fact. What's more, the latest polls I've seen indicate that the vast majority of Americans know this to be true. Nearly 90 percent of Americans believe in God.[2] But despite the fact that God isn't dead, despite the fact that the majority of us believe that to be true, why do so many Americans seem to continue down the road of their isms? Why do so many continue toward death and destruction?

I suppose the Devil makes them do it.

Time presented Friedrich Nietzsche's thesis, the thesis that "self-centered man had killed God, and that settled that." Here's what Nietzsche failed to realize: that declaration was far from settled. Here's what else he failed to realize: if the God of the Bible is dead, man has no hope of experiencing eternal life. Of course, Nietzsche discovered that truth just after he took his last breath. Nanoseconds after crossing over death's threshold, the German philosopher stood at the judgment seat of the wild, fearsome Lord of the universe, the living God.

It's been forty-three years since my encounter with God, and I can tell you, I'm not running from anyone or anything; I'm not enslaved to the isms of the world. And if America would awaken to that same truth, the truth and good news Jesus came to bring us, it might just change everything. In this book I aim to show you this very thing.

There's a lot of bad news today. Suicide rates are up. Abortion runs rampant. Acts of terrorism plague the world. But once you understand how bad the bad news is, you'll appreciate the good news—and it's really good. Once you appreciate the bad news, you'll have the ability to truly adore the good news. What is that good news? Follow me. Come and see.

THE LIE: GOD IS DEAD.

THE TRUTH: THE GOD OF THE BIBLE IS NOT DEAD AND HE NEVER WILL BE.

I watched Miss Kay's Volkswagen Bug pull from the trailer and disappear. She'd taken whatever household items she could—some kitchen utensils, a few pots and pans, three folding lawn chairs, the black-and-white television—and stuffed them into the trunk. She'd loaded the boys into their seats and crammed their clothes and keepsakes around them. She'd even taken their toothbrushes.

Miss Kay, my wife of only a few years, was leaving. Maybe for good.

Before the fight that resulted in me showing Miss Kay the door, I'd been at home alone with the boys: Alan, Jason, and Willie. I was sitting on the porch, fuming while I waited to go out with my friends per my usual routine. As I sat and stewed, and the seconds ticked by, I grew more restless. I'd already started drinking and was about half-lit when Miss Kay finally walked through the front door.

"You're late," I said. "Again."

She apologized and blamed it on work, but I thought I knew better, and I told her so. I accused her of running around on me. I accused her of lying to cover it up. I was sure she was a cheater, I said, and though there was no real evidence to bolster my accusation,

I was convinced. And what was most upsetting, her running around had disrupted my night. It had interfered with my plans for freedom and fun, my fishing, drinking, and carousing in the woods on State Line Road. This was the last time.

The argument escalated. So did my voice. And that's when I said the words that triggered a series of life-altering events, the words that would eventually open the door of God's grace to me.

"You're ruining my life!" I roared.

"You've been ruining my life for ten years!" she yelled back.

"Get out," I said, pointing to the door, "and take your kids with you!" As if they weren't my kids too.

Miss Kay shook from head to toe while she gathered what she could as fast as she could. Still, she knew this was the end of the line. She didn't grovel. She didn't beg. She was resolved to give me exactly what I'd asked for. In less than an hour she'd disappeared into a Louisiana rainstorm. I stood in that rain and watched her go, and there, in that moment, I had no remorse. I thought I'd fixed my problem. I thought I was finally free.

Of course, a fight of this magnitude isn't made in a moment or a day or even a month. This last standoff between Miss Kay and me grew from years of unrest. What was the source of that unrest? I suppose I thought Miss Kay was cramping my style. I needed freedom, and for so many years, I'd been busy chasing some version of it. Freedom from the structure. Freedom from the law. Freedom from the rules. And there'd been so many rules.

I'd been reared by a God-fearing mother and father, and for as long as I can remember, they had me in church. I attended my fair share of Sunday morning services at my country Church of Christ, heard sermon after sermon for eighteen years. I took Communion, drank the grape juice, and ate the stale crackers. I heard message after message about what it meant to be a member of the church. "Hear, believe, repent, confess, and be baptized," they said, but what any of it meant was beyond me. It was religious talk, mumbo jumbo. All I knew for sure was that I was supposed to follow the rules— don't drink; don't cuss; don't dance. I was supposed to behave like the church folks, even if behaving wasn't my strong suit. And it wasn't.

Miss Kay and I met while I was in high school, and we'd fallen in love. She was a good girl with a beautiful smile, and her home life was an utter disaster. When she was fourteen, her father suffered a massive heart attack and died. All that grief derailed everything, and for a time, her mother was checked out, absent. Miss Kay needed saving, I thought; what's more, I was just the man to save her. I genuinely loved her and wanted to spend the rest of my life with her. So, when we discovered Miss Kay was pregnant with our first child, Al, we had what we referred to as a "pioneer wedding" in the summer of 1964. It was a brief exchange of vows. No minister. No marriage certificate. It'd be 1968 before we'd call a justice of the peace and make it legal, but in those days, our pioneer wedding was enough for us.

I'd been offered a scholarship to play on the football team at Louisiana Tech University. So, in the fall of that same year, Miss Kay and I packed up what little we had, and we made our way to Ruston, Louisiana. The sixties were in full swing when we arrived on campus; it was the height of the hippie movement. Only months earlier

Time had asked the question "Is God Dead?" And within days of starting classes, I realized my professors had already reached their own conclusions: God was, in fact, dead, and so man was free. Free to party. Free to join the sexual revolution. Free to be whoever he wanted to be. Free to chase happiness.

I sat in those classes semester after semester. Psychology classes. Biology classes. Philosophy classes. And because I'd never heard the good news of the living God, I began to buy what these professors were selling. If it were true, if God was dead, shouldn't I be free to chase my own happiness?

I graduated college by the skin of my teeth in 1969 and entered the master of education program at Louisiana Tech that same year. That fall I began teaching English and coaching sports in Junction City, Arkansas, while I took my master's classes at night. At Junction City I met Big Al Bolen on the first day of school. He was a large man with an even larger intellect, and his appetite for a good party was even larger still. He was a science teacher and an atheist and, for whatever reason, we took a shine to each other from the start. I'd never been much of a partier before I met Big Al, but I was drawn to the kind of freedom he seemed to embody. We were inseparable in my days at Junction City, and he invited me into his rowdy lifestyle.

We'd teach during the day and raise hell during the night. On the weekends we'd be the last ones out of the bar, and we'd take off for the river or the woods to run trotlines and poach. We'd meet up with a small band of miscreants just off the beaten path, and we'd get high, get drunk, and get laid, mostly in that order. I did it all despite the fact that I was a husband and a father.

For the first time I was tasting what I thought was freedom—the drugs, the drinking, the sleeping around. With each passing night I indulged a little more. For a time that indulgence felt so good. It was a lifestyle I'd never experienced, but as is the Robertson way, I took to it like a duck to water.

As the years wore on, my behavior became more erratic and unruly. My partying began to spill into the week; I was losing control. On many occasions I'd come through the trailer door after a night of partying, and there'd be Miss Kay, tending the children and waiting on me. So often I'd shift the blame; I'd light into her and accuse her of her own infidelities, of sleeping around. The irony was not lost on her, and she'd protest, tell me that she was too busy working and raising our passel of boys to cheat. (Willie had joined the family in 1972.) She was trying her best to hold the family together, she said. What's more, she knew I was guilty of my own indiscretions, and she did not shy away from confronting me.

"Why are you acting this way? Why don't you come home and be with your family?"

"I just need my freedom," I told her.

"Is this freedom? Really?"

Miss Kay was right. I didn't know what true freedom was.

As I wrote in *Happy, Happy, Happy*, my days of debauchery reached their height in 1975. I'd lost my job as a high school teacher the year before. As if that wasn't enough, I'd managed a bar after that stint as a high school teacher and coach. And though it'd been a successful business venture, I'd lost it all in a violent dispute and resulting fist fight with the property owners. The owners had shut-tered the bar. They'd pressed charges too. I went on the run.

A fugitive from the law, I was flat broke. Needing employment, I took a job on an offshore rig in the Gulf of Mexico, and in the between times, I hid out in the woods and partied with Big Al and the gang while Miss Kay sorted out my legal troubles. I was shirking responsibilities, controlled by my own desires. The desire to drink. The desire for women. The desire to do what I wanted to do. But the more I chased my desires, the emptier I felt. And with this real-ization, a deep guilt set in.

The guilt was the thing that led to my outburst with Miss Kay that night in the trailer. It was the source of my fury, my anger, even my jealousy. Thinking it was my family who caused all the guilt, who kept me from experiencing ultimate freedom, I could only see one solution. I had to get rid of them. Maybe by pushing them away, I thought, I'd push the guilt away too.

After Miss Kay pulled away from the trailer in her VW, I decided to make the most of my newfound freedom. I'd live it up. I'd work when I wanted, hunt and fish when I wanted. I'd drink what I wanted, when I wanted, and with whomever I wanted. For a week or so I did just that. I lived in my own bachelor's paradise. But it didn't take long for the truth to set in: my ideal bachelor's paradise was no kind of paradise at all. In fact, it was a prison of guilt, shame, and loneliness. Why didn't I feel a new sense of freedom? What had gone wrong?

I didn't have the benefit of the Scriptures in those days. No one had taught me the plain truth: God was not dead. He was alive, and he'd written his law, the law of right and wrong, on my heart. I didn't know that my guilt was a result of violating the very real law of a very real and living God. I didn't know the words of Paul:

> When Gentiles, who do not have the law, do by nature things required by the law, they are a law for themselves, even though they do not have the law. They show that the requirements of the law are written on their hearts, their consciences also bearing witness, and their thoughts sometimes accusing them and at other times even defending them. (Rom. 2:14–15)

Had I known the Word of God, maybe I would have understood that by choosing to violate God's law, I'd chosen judgment under the law. In that judgment I'd condemned myself to my own prison of guilt and shame. If I had known the truth, maybe I would have understood why my conscience ached and why I felt so isolated and alone. But I didn't. And so even with Miss Kay and the kids gone, even in the absence of responsibility, even in my bachelor's paradise, I couldn't escape my misery. Hunting, fishing, and partying had all lost their luster. I was ten times more a prisoner after Miss Kay left, and I knew it within the first week.

Little did I know, in those months, Miss Kay had her own encounter with the living God. She'd always believed in him, but after she left me, she went all in. She'd given everything in her life to him, and somewhere, miles away from my trailer prison, she was praying. She was praying I'd be miserable in my sin. She was praying that misery would drive me into the arms of God. She was praying that God would reconcile our marriage, our family. Miss Kay was praying for my freedom.

I think it was the power of those prayers that wouldn't let me wallow in my misery for more than a month. And when that misery became too much to bear, and when I came to understand how empty my life was, I slid into the driver's seat of my truck, hungover as I was. Miss Kay was working at Howard Brothers in Monroe, Louisiana, at the time, and so I set off to find her. I held the steering wheel in some kind of a death grip as I drove into town, hands trembling from nerves and engine vibrations.

I cried from the minute I hit the city limits to the time I pulled into the store parking lot. I bawled, in fact—a thing I'd been too proud to do for most of my life. In that parking lot I sat in my truck, engine idling, head on my steering wheel, wondering what I'd say to Miss Kay if she even agreed to see me. But before I could get up the nerve to open the truck door, there she was, tapping on my window. I rolled it down.

She was as rigid as a pecan tree, looked as sturdy as one too. She didn't say anything at first. She just stood there, staring. I broke the silence.

"I can't sleep. I can't eat. I'm miserable," I told her. "I just want my family back."

I was the one who groveled first. Those are the facts.

"I'll quit drinking this time," I said, but I could tell she didn't believe me. It was a hollow promise, one I'd made too many times before.

"No," she said. "Promises aren't enough, Phil. You need help."

She was right. The truth was, I couldn't any more get myself sober than Big Al could stop being big. Agreeing with Miss Kay's assessment, I remembered the only man who'd ever had the guts to try to teach me something about God during my partying years. His name was Bill, and he was the preacher from my sister's church. Years ago, before I lost the beer joint outside of Junction City, he'd waltzed in with my sister and offered to teach me the good news of God. I, of course, had refused to hear it.

"Think you could find that preacher who had enough guts to come to the bar a few months back?"

She nodded and said she'd been going to his church for the last several months. She gave me the address to her apartment and asked me to meet her there at five o'clock. The preacher, Bill Smith, would be there, she said.

That night Bill sat across from me at Miss Kay's makeshift dinner table—a small card table that almost didn't fit in her tiny apartment—and he asked a pointed question.

"Do you know the gospel?"

I stared at him, and I reckon my look said all he needed to know.

"What do you think of when you hear the word *gospel*, Phil?"

"I don't know," I said. "The Chuck Wagon Gang? Gospel music?"

"Do you know the good news?" he asked.

The good news of what? I'd been to church for the first eighteen years of my life, I told him, but I'd never really heard what could be called *good news*. I'd only been told the stories of the Old Testament characters, maybe a few things about instrumental music and church structure. I'd been told I needed to hear, believe, repent, confess, and be baptized, but every time I heard this formula, I was left thinking, *Hear what? Believe what? Repent from what? Confess what?* No, I told Bill, to the best of my recollection I'd never heard any good news in church. Instead, I was given a do-right formula, and the sad truth was, I never felt like I could do right. I wasn't good enough.

"I see," he said. "Can I tell you the best news you've ever heard?"

I nodded.

"Do you trust me?"

"I don't trust anyone."

He smiled. "I wouldn't either, not considering the fellas you've been running around with."

He pointed to the Bible on the table next to him.

"Do you trust this?" he asked.

"Sure, I trust it. But my father told me never to take a man's word at face value, especially about the Bible. You can share your story of the Bible with me, Mr. Preacher Man, but you should know I'm going to read every verse you quote for myself, so you'd better give it to me straight."

"Fair enough," Bill said before pulling a folded restaurant napkin from his pocket. He drew a series of hieroglyphs on that napkin. First, he drew an arrow pointing down. Then a cross. Next a half circle. Then an arrow pointing up. Finally, he drew an arrow pointing down.

$$\downarrow \quad \dagger \quad \cap \quad \uparrow \quad \downarrow$$

"Let's keep it simple," he said, then he shared how God made man for fellowship, but how man broke God's law. As a consequence, men had been separated from God ever since. "But God never wanted that separation," he said, "and so he made a way."

He pointed to the first arrow and explained how the God who created the universe loved man enough to step into that creation. Jesus was God's very Word made flesh, he said, and Jesus came and lived among his people. He healed the sick, made the lame walk, and brought provision to the poor. That same Jesus preached the ultimate good news: those who followed him would be free from sin and guilt and would have an eternal home with him.

Bill pointed to the cross he'd drawn on the napkin, then explained how Jesus' teachings made the religious folks angry. In fact, Jesus made the rulers so angry they nailed him to a cross. Here's what they didn't know: when Jesus went to the cross, he took on the sins of the whole world, even the sins of those religious rulers who crucified him. He took on the penalty of our separation.

He paused and asked if I was following. I told him I was, and he pointed to the semicircle, the dome. After his death Jesus was laid in a tomb, Bill said. He pointed to the next arrow, the arrow pointing up, and he laid out the scriptures showing how Jesus conquered death, how he rose from the dead. The final arrow showed how Christ would return for those who believed.

"He's coming back for his people, for those who've trusted in his death, burial, and resurrection," Bill said. "Then he'll take us home to live with him in eternity."

I sat there, stunned. I'd gone to church for years. How had I missed this? God could forgive me? He could free me from sin and guilt, even with all the things I'd done? He'd allow me to live in eternity with him? It was the most compelling story I'd ever heard. This was truly good news!

He finished his mini-sermon and asked me what I thought.

"I've never heard anything like it," I said, then I gave him the hardest look I could muster. "I'm going to read every verse you gave me, and if you're not telling the truth, I'll know it. If it doesn't add up, we're done."

Unfazed, he nodded and then asked me whether I'd be willing to meet with him the following evening. I told him I would.

That same night I reviewed the scriptures he'd referenced. I read the first chapter of the Gospel of John, and sure enough, there it was. The very living God—the God who was surely not dead— came to earth in the form of Jesus. I read of his life, his death, and his resurrection. In Paul's writings I came to understand that Jesus had died as a sacrifice for my sins. It was this sacrifice that made a way for me (1 Cor. 15:3–5).

I read the promises of John, how choosing to be in fellowship with Jesus would free me from all sins—past, present, and future. Finally, in the book of Acts, I read the ultimate promise. Jesus would return for everyone who believed in him.

Sure enough, the story was just as Bill said. The Bible showed how God was very much alive, and how he made a way for forgiveness of my sin. He could free me of all my guilt and could solve my ultimate problem—death. The notion of freedom from guilt and death filled me with great peace, a peace of mind I'd never experienced. I knew this story was the solution to all my problems. It was the solution to my disorienting drunkenness, my promiscuity, my search for freedom. And the more I considered it, the more I came to see that it satisfied a deep spiritual longing I didn't even know I had.

I met with Bill the next evening and told him I'd done my homework. I'd reviewed every scripture he gave me, and sure enough, his story panned out. It was the greatest story I'd ever heard, I said, and I wanted to follow this Jesus. I wanted to be baptized.

That night, in a near-empty auditorium with Bill Smith, Miss Kay, and my three boys, I gave my confession of faith. I believed in the saving work of Jesus and wanted to be free of sin and guilt. I wanted to follow him in baptism. Down into the water I went, and when I came up from that cleansing flood, I knew I was a changed man. Somehow, in that water, I'd encountered God. And that was the moment I decided I'd share the good news of Jesus with anyone God put in my path.

I stepped out of that baptistery, made my way to Miss Kay and the boys, and gave each of them a soggy hug. There was a new joy in this embrace with Miss Kay; a shift was already happening. The peace and strength I'd seen in Miss Kay over those last two days began to fill me too. Everything seemed so much lighter. And though I wasn't sure how I'd stay on the straight and narrow, shaky as I was, I figured God would make a way. Wasn't this the promise of all those scriptures I'd studied?

Years later Bill Smith told me that our meeting at Miss Kay's apartment convinced him to begin sharing the good news of God through that same little diagram he showed me. He called it "The Witness," and for years he carried it with him everywhere he went. The church had it translated into multiple languages, and missionaries shared it around the world. It's proven to be a powerful tool and, following Bill's example, I still share it with anyone God brings to me: the rich, the poor, the powerless and powerful.

In 2016, just before the presidential election, I had the privilege of meeting with then presidential nominee Donald Trump in Washington, DC, at the Values Voter Summit. There I asked whether I could share some good news with him. He agreed, and I pulled out a copy of The Witness I'd drawn on a card.

"Whether you win or lose, don't miss this," I said. "This is the most important thing you'll ever hear."

I explained the diagram and shared how the living God had made a way for us to have fellowship with him. I shared the truth of Jesus, of his death, burial, resurrection, and ascension. I shared how belief in Jesus might free him from all his past and future sins. I shared how he might come to live for eternity. When I finished, I looked up at him, wondering what he might say.

He pointed to the diagram, which I'd placed on his desk. "Can I have that?" he asked. I handed it to him, and he folded it up and put it in his pocket.

I don't know if President Trump had ever heard the truth of God before that day, and I don't know whether he has accepted the message I shared with him. But here's what I know: like all of us,

God has written the truth of his law on the president's heart. And so, sooner or later (if he hasn't already), I pray that God sees fit to lead him into that truth. I hope President Trump has a freeing encounter with the God who is most certainly alive, the God who cannot be killed by human hands.

If there's one thing I know, it's this: an encounter with the living God is the only hope for mankind. It's the only hope for President Trump, for me, for America. It's the only hope for true freedom and lasting peace. And the God of the universe has made a way for us to have this kind of encounter. That way is Jesus, the very personification of God, the very hope of the world.

The personification—the one men believed they killed—defeated death. He is alive, no matter what the professors, psychologists, and scientists say.

2

THE LIE: THERE IS NO DEVIL.

THE TRUTH: THE DEVIL OF THE BIBLE
IS REAL AND HE IS OUR ENEMY.

In the moments after my baptism, after that soggy hug with Miss Kay, we stood outside the church building. There Miss Kay told me what Jason had said.

She said, "Jason asked, 'Does this mean the Devil doesn't live in Daddy anymore?'"

With what I'd just experienced, I couldn't deny that the Devil was very real and that he'd had me under his spell. But how did Jason already know about him?

"What did you tell him?"

She took my hands and smiled. She'd told Jason the Devil had been driven from me, but it didn't mean it'd be smooth sailing. I'd still be rough around the edges, she told him. Rough edges. I suppose that was the kindest way to describe me. But Miss Kay assured me she'd take all my rough edges. She was just glad to have her family back.

The Devil, that father of lies who'd convinced me I needed my freedom, was gone. I could almost feel him leaving my body, my trailer, my land. In an instant my penchant for drinking, getting high, and cheating on Miss Kay had evaporated. My road of self-destruction and death had been rerouted. Newly soaked with the waters of a physical and spiritual baptism, I'd been set on the straight-and-narrow, and for the first time in my life, I really wanted to be good. But how is a bad man supposed to be good? Can you teach an old river rat new tricks?

I figured there was only one way to change my lifestyle. I'd need to shun all those lies I'd believed and walk into the truth. To do that, I needed space. I needed separation from those old boys who were running buddies with the Devil himself. But even though I knew what I needed to do, my life of new faith was not without setbacks.

In the first month of my conversion, one of my old buddies came along and asked me to go fishing with him. Fishing with an old friend in the middle of the afternoon couldn't hurt anything, could it? I asked him whether there was water in his cooler, and he said there was. With that, we were off.

An hour into our fishing expedition, with the Louisiana sun beating down on our boat, I went for the water. To my surprise, I discovered that he'd only brought a couple of six packs of beer. (Should I have been surprised? Liars lie, after all.) It was midday, and humidity had sucked every ounce of moisture from me. What was a thirsty man supposed to do? Couldn't I drink a beer or two and be fine? So I grabbed a can, pulled the tab, and drank.

Then I pulled the tab on another can.

Then another.

A few hours, a mess of catfish, and too many beers later, we headed back. When I stumbled back into the trailer, there was Miss Kay, sitting in her rocker and chatting with my parents who'd come for an unexpected visit. She knew in an instant, but she asked anyway.

"Have you been drinking again?"

"It was all he had," I said, half-lit as I stumbled to the bedroom.

I don't remember the crash landing, but I remember waking up hungover. It was Sunday, and when it came time to get ready for church, I told Miss Kay I didn't feel well. I'd rather stay home, I told her, and she capitulated at first. My mother, though, was not having a lick of it. She marched into my room, stared me down, and said, "Phil, get up. You're going to church."

That settled that.

I sat through that church service, ashamed that I'd been tricked into drinking. I don't remember the sermon. I don't remember the songs we sang. I do remember the sense of conviction that plagued me throughout the service. I knew the truth—the truth that had set me free—and yet I'd fallen into the schemes of an untrustworthy friend. I'd fallen for the lie.

Near the end of the service, Bill Smith stood and offered an invitation to repent and turn to Jesus, and before the first bar of the first song was sung, I started making my way to the front. Bill met me there, and I told him I'd managed to get commode-hugging drunk the day before. He received my confession with more grace than I deserved, and after the invitation song was sung, he stood and shared my struggle with the congregation. To my great amazement, no one heaped judgment or shame on me. In fact, there was nothing but acceptance and love. An elderly lady, one I'd never met, came to me and said, "I love you, and I'm proud of you." Another approached me and said, "God forgives you. That's what the grace of God is all about. Get up and keep walking."

When I walked out of church that morning, I knew I had to double down on my efforts to escape Satan's snares. How could I go back to running with the good ol' boys? Weren't they living under the influence of the evil one? Weren't they the ones who led me into the prison of my own desires? Didn't they want to lure me back to those old haunts, the places that were devoid of peace? And this new family, this family of God, weren't they more gracious and loving than any of my old running buddies?

I'd spent twenty-eight years under the influence of Satan. I knew it'd take time to untangle all those lies, and you can't untangle the lies of the Devil when you're running with his children. I knew what I needed to do, and I entered a self-imposed sort of holy witness protection program. We'd already moved, and the boys from Junction City didn't know where I was living. I changed my phone number. I cut off communication with the men who'd trained me to follow my own desires. I stopped running around with Big Al and the crew once and for all. I lived like a recluse, almost as if I were in hiding for the first three months.

In those reclusive days, Bill invited me to a Bible study with a rather prolific group of well-known sinners. In that study he taught us the truth about sin and the father of sin. The Devil, he said, was the father of lies, and he was prowling, looking for an opening to steal us back. He taught us that the only way to combat the lies of Satan was to devote ourselves to the study of Scripture and to allow God to speak through its pages.

And so I devoted the majority of my waking hours to studying the Bible. I pored over the onion-skin pages and began to mark them up. I consumed the Word of God as if it were food and drank deeply from its waters of wisdom. As I read and read and read, I saw the truth about the human condition: every last one of us has been infected by sin; every last one of us is under the influence of the evil one.

As Miss Kay and I righted the ship of our marriage, I decided I needed to leave the oil fields and put my education to work. I had two college degrees and classroom experience, but I'd lost my teaching job in Junction City on account of my wayward lifestyle. What's more, I had a record with the law, a thing that doesn't earn you any points with high school administrators when you're looking to steer the lives of the town's youth. But, resolved to make good, I went to my new church family and asked them to put in a good word. Bill Smith reached out to contacts he had at a Christian school in Ouachita Parish, and though they would not hire me for a permanent position, they allowed me to substitute teach. I worked hard, did the best I could, and before long I was hired as coach and literature teacher at Ouachita Christian School.

Things were changing. The power of God was active in my life. This power was awakening me to the truth of the gospel: in Jesus I could beat sin and death; in Jesus I could have a new life. It stripped me of my desire to go back to my old partying ways, sure. Even more, it set me on a path of understanding. And in that understanding, an unquenchable desire to free others began to grow in me.

In that *Time* article from 1966, the German theologian Heinz Zahrnt addressed the question, "Is God dead?" clarifying "What is in question is God himself." If God himself is in question, isn't Satan in question too? If God is dead, what about the Devil?

There can be no doubt that the world would try to convince us that the Devil is dead, but it's a specious argument, one based on circular reasoning. Both Scripture and my own personal experience undercut this argument. Truth is, my life attests: Satan, the father of all lies, the chief prevaricator, is very much alive. Truth is, he'd rather have you believe that he's dead, inactive, or a myth if it'd keep you out of the arms of God.

The question of God—who first posed it? You know the story of Genesis, how God planted a garden and set a man named Adam in the middle of it. From Adam's rib he cut a woman and named her Eve. As the story goes, God gave Adam and Eve full rule over the garden, with only one restriction. They could not eat of the tree in the center of the garden, the Tree of the Knowledge of Good and Evil. If they did, God said, they would die. Seems simple enough, right?

Enter the Devil.

Taking the form of a serpent, the vile liar visited Eve and tempted her first with a question: "God told you not to eat from that tree?" Eve responded and said God had warned them that if they ate from the tree, mankind would be finished. That's when the first lie entered the ears of a human. "But the serpent said to the woman,

'You will not die. For God knows that when you eat of it your eyes will be opened, and you will be like God, knowing good and evil'" (Gen. 3:4–5 RSV). You can set yourself free of God, the Devil intimated; you can kill him and become your own god.

Sound familiar?

Eve was tricked by the Devil's lies, and what was the result of that trick? Sin entered the world, and with it, an endless cycle of death and destruction. Into the world came drunkenness. Into the world came sexual immorality and perversion. Into the world came wars and rumors of wars. Into the world came violence and racial divide. The world was forever changed because of the crafty lies spun by a slithering serpent. Those lies have slithered on throughout history.

In the Gospels that record the life of Jesus, we see the Devil, still scheming, still spinning the same sorts of lies. In the eighth chapter of John, Jesus was speaking to the people, and some religious leaders were in the crowd. Jesus—a man known for saying it like it was—spoke the truth, said that every last one of them had been born into sin slavery. There was good news, though. He'd come to bring freedom, and if they followed his command, they'd be free indeed. That's when the story turned. He turned to the religious leaders and uncovered their hidden motivation. They'd not come for freedom, he said; they'd come to kill him. But how did he know?

"I am telling you what I have seen in the Father's presence," he said, "and you are doing what you have heard from your father." As if to remove all doubt about who the father of the religious leaders was, Jesus spoke even more plainly. "If God were your Father, you would love me, for I have come here from God. . . . You belong to your father, the devil, and you want to carry out your father's desires. He was a murderer from the beginning" (John 8:38, 42, 44).

Jesus outed the truth. The Devil was alive and active, and he controlled the desires of the religious leaders of the day. What was the chief aim of the Devil, and consequently, what was the chief aim of the religious leaders? Murder. Murder Jesus. Murder God.

Murder, death, destruction—these are Satan's chief means of separating humans from God. Can't you see his work all around you? Hasn't it run amok in America? Suicide rates are at an all-time high.[1] Somewhere between 40 and 50 percent of marriages die in divorce.[2] Hundreds of thousands of babies are aborted annually.[3] America is a slaughterhouse. Why? We've been enslaved by the power of the evil one, the murderer of all murderers.

But look here: if Satan can't kill you immediately, he has other tools at his disposal. He'll imprison you in your own desires or use your intellect against you until you go down to death. Drugs, alcohol, illicit sex, greed, false beliefs (like "God is dead")—these are among the tools Satan uses to keep us in bondage, to keep us from experiencing the freedom of God's kingdom before we take our last breath. Paul is clear about the tools of Satan, the tools he calls "the works of the flesh":

> Now the works of the flesh are evident, which are: adultery, fornication, uncleanness, lewdness, idolatry, sorcery, hatred, contentions, jealousies, outbursts of wrath, selfish ambitions, dissensions, heresies, envy, murders, drunkenness, revelries, and

the like; of which I tell you beforehand, just as I also told you in time past, that those who practice such things will not inherit the kingdom of God. (Gal. 5:19–21 NKJV)

Scripture is likewise clear about the primary influencer of our works of the flesh, our sins. As John wrote, "He who sins is of the devil, for the devil has sinned from the beginning" (1 John 3:8 NKJV). And his temptations toward sin aren't just random or willy-nilly. He operates a highly organized crime syndicate, a ring of demons whose only goal is to pull us toward desire, and ultimately, destruction. As Paul reminds us, "Our struggle is not against flesh and blood, but against the rulers, against the authorities, against the powers of this dark world and against the spiritual forces of evil in the heavenly realms" (Eph. 6:12).

Look around, America. Don't you see Satan's influence at work around you? The entertainment industry mocks religion and celebrates perversity. Universities teach the death of God and Satan with scientific precision. Physicians and psychologists tell us that when we die, the lights go out forever. Sin, the works of our flesh—can there be any question that Satan is alive and well in our country? And when you remove Christ from the public square, from courthouses and schools, when you bar truth from its institutions, should it come as a surprise that the Devil steps in to fill the void? Consider historical examples.

Consider Hitler. Some estimates indicate he killed six million Jews and committed numerous war atrocities. Where was Jesus in the Nazi regime? Nowhere.

Remember Stalin and the Communists? They banished Jesus and subsequently became famous for murder.

What about ISIS? There's no Jesus in their midst, and what's their regime known for? Beheadings. Burnings. Rape. Murder. Death. Destruction.

As long as women keep birthing babies, as long as the human race continues to walk the earth, as long as the power of God allows, the Devil will be in business. Unchecked by the truth of Jesus, Satan is free to work his agenda—death. This agenda can take down a person, sure; this agenda can take down entire countries too.

There are two powers at war on this planet: the power of the living God and the power of the living Satan. One of those powers—the power of Satan—has been allowed to remain active on the earth, but only for a time. Ultimately, the power of God will rid the world of his lies. How do I know? The Scriptures tell us as much. As John wrote, "For this purpose the Son of God was manifested, that He might destroy the works of the devil" (1 John 3:8 NKJV). As followers of Christ, our duty is to expose Satan and his agenda. It's our mission to warn our family, our friends, and our country of the death and destruction he brings. It's time to point to the snake tracks in the ground, to tell the people that as followers of Christ, we have the antivenin.

As I began to grow in my knowledge of Christ, as the lies of the Devil were exposed, I began to sense my time of witness protection was coming to a close. Before long the Christian needs to get busy, needs to respond to his mission. He needs to speak the truth of Christ to a dying world. I was no exception.

Within a year Big Al had managed to track me down. (He was a crafty redneck.) He rolled up in the yard one afternoon with a couple of old buddies. He said they were going to State Line Road to party and promised it'd be a grand time. I knew better, knew the way that lie would turn out; I'd wind up drunk, hanging over a toilet, full of guilt and shame, unable to look my church family in the eye. So I told Big Al and the gang I wouldn't be joining them. He frowned and asked if I was on some sort of a religious kick.

"I believe this is something more than a religious kick," I said. "Boys, this is permanent."

They didn't mock me, didn't belittle me. They just stood there, confused.

"The one you're looking for," I told them, referring to the old Phil Robertson, "he's dead."

The old gang stood there perplexed, but Big Al did not hesitate to share his opinion. He said I couldn't stay committed to this nonsense of Jesus, and then for added effect, he said, "When all this is over, Phil, give me a call."

From time to time over those following years, a few of the dudes would come around. Time and time again, they'd make big promises of fun and freedom, promises I knew they couldn't fulfill. I stuck with my story, told them I'd given up that lifestyle. I'd decided to follow my Father, I said, the Father of truth. Over those years I stuck to my story, and some of them began to believe. Not Big Al, though, at least not until the end.

Twelve years after my conversion, the phone rang.

"I need to talk with you."

It was Big Al.

"Can you come up to Junction City?"

I hung up the phone, told Miss Kay that I thought his time had come. I made my way north to Arkansas, and the two of us met on the banks of the river. He stood there, softer than I'd ever remembered him.

"I've been keeping up with you," he said, "and I must admit, I've never seen such a change in a man." He looked down, kicked at the pine needles on the ground, and then said, "Guess what my doctor told me?"

"What?" I asked.

"It looks like I have an aneurysm in my heart that could burst at any moment."

I sized him up and then asked, "So, are you having second thoughts about your atheism?"

Big Al nodded, then asked me what had made such a difference in my life. How had I changed? I relayed my conversion story, shared how I'd been a prisoner of the Devil and how God had freed me from that prison. I shared the death, burial, and resurrection of Jesus and the death, burial, and resurrection of Phil Robertson. I told him that the Devil had enslaved him through his own desires, but that God wanted to free him from that bondage. I gave him the unfiltered truth of God, shared the good news of Jesus with him, and when I was finished, I waited for his response.

"I tell you what," he said, "because of this aneurysm, I don't know if I'm going to make it. This story, if it's true, it changes everything. I reckon I underestimated it."

That was an understatement.

"Think you could take me down to the river and baptize me?"

"Yes," I said, and that's just what we did.

Two months later I received a phone call from Big Al's wife. His aneurysm had burst, and he was gone. Before he passed he'd shared one last request. He wanted me to preach at his funeral. So, more than twelve years after I'd been run out of Junction City for being a no-good heathen, I showed up in plain clothes to preach Al's funeral. Come to find out, Big Al had become quite the figure in Junction City, and the whole town showed up for his funeral. It was a packed house. But how many of the congregants knew the truth of Al's life? How many knew about his conversion?

"Let me tell you a story about the man in the casket," I said. "His body is there, but he's gone. A couple of months ago, I had the privilege of baptizing Al into the family of Christ. He cut it thin," I said, "but he made it."

There was a near-audible gasp, and many in the room began to cry. I shared the story, and in that story I laid out the good news of Jesus. I told them that Jesus wanted to set them free, just like he had Al. When I'd finished my remarks, I looked out at the audience. There was not a dry eye. Before leaving the stage, I looked down in the casket.

"My old buddy, I'll see you again."

Al, the staunchest atheist I'd ever met, had unwound the lies of the Devil before the end. He'd been freed from Satan's power, freed from the power of death too. He'd become a child of God.

Big Al could be a testament to America, if only we'd hear it. Sure, we might be under the spell of the Devil; we might be tangled up in his lies. We might celebrate violence and drunkenness and sex and drugs, success, wealth, scientific advancement—anything really. But if we face our own mortality, if we come to see that without Jesus we're on the road to eternal death—just as I did, just as Big Al did—we can come into a new season of freedom. That freedom, though, won't come without an awakening, without an infusion of absolute truth, and this is the absolute truth—the real and living God wants to free us from death; he wants to free us to flourish.

THE LIE: TRUTH IS RELATIVE.

THE TRUTH: THERE IS ABSOLUTE
TRUTH AND IT COMES FROM GOD.

The power of God—who knew it could change a river rat's heart? Knowing my own fragility, I gave myself to this power the best way I knew how. I committed to reading the Bible every day. I treated it as if it were bread and water, and the only way I could eat and drink it was through my eyes and ears.

I was utterly desperate for the Scriptures. In the mornings I read before the boys awoke. Between classes I'd pull a copy from my desk drawer and wade into it. After one of Miss Kay's famous home-cooked meals, after the boys were bathed, after they'd settled in for the night, I'd settle into reading the Word. I read it so much, I inadvertently began committing certain passages to memory. It turns out, the Bible was the truth, and the truth was setting me free.

When I wasn't immersed in the Scriptures, I was immersed in the things of God at church. I continued to attend the Bible study with those reformed bandits, the river rats and rednecks who'd accepted Christ just like I had. But as I grew into my faith, as I rooted into church like a backwater cypress, I met other men, men of repute like Tommy Powell, Doyle Jennings, Bill Johnson, Lynn Campbell, and J. J. Turner, who wanted nothing more than to advance God's agenda on the earth. Their commitment to living upright lives in accordance with the truth of God's Word had led to success, and I figured I could learn something from them. So I attended their Bible classes and hung on their every word. They became my big brothers in the faith, and they showed me how their commitment to the absolute truth of the Scriptures had led to their success. This is not to say they were all wealthy, of course, but they had everything they needed. More than that, they were free.

As I surveyed the good churchmen around me, I noted how they'd been blessed. Best as I could tell, they'd been found trustworthy enough to be blessed by God, and they shared those blessings with the community. Trustworthiness—*what a deal.*

Before God had wrestled me out of the muddy banks of the Ouachita, I was the most untrustworthy redneck. I was all about the party, all about whoring around. I was all about poaching ducks and running the back roads drunk. Restraint was boredom. Law-abiding was its own prison cell. I lied when I had to. Cheated too. My desire drove me, and I made my own rules, set my own boundaries. The truth was relative, at least as far as I was concerned. But that was before the truth of Jesus came calling, before it showed me that my lack of restraint was the real prison, a prison of death. And now that I'd come to believe, I wanted to be found faithful, trustworthy.

I found the profession of teaching to be very kind to me in those early years of faith. It was a good job, and it gave Miss Kay and the boys the financial stability they needed. It allowed me to influence and pour into the young men of Northern Louisiana, too, and that felt good. But even as my students and the administrators grew more and more comfortable with having a country boy with a master's degree in the classroom, I was growing more uncomfortable. I felt the pull of God's creation, the call of the river. (You can take a rat out of the river, but I don't suppose you can ever take the river out of the rat.) I felt the tug of business, and the business I wanted more than anything was to make duck calls.

Was it a crazy idea? Probably.

Would God provide? I figured he would.

How'd I know? I believed the truth of God's Word.

In my time devouring the Scriptures, I'd read that God provides for his children. I took God's promise in the Proverbs to heart, how he'd never let his children go hungry (10:3). I read the Psalms and noted his promise to satisfy the thirsty and give good food to his children (107:9). I read the writings of Paul and believed what he told the Philippians, namely, "God will meet all your needs according to the riches of his glory in Christ Jesus" (4:19). I read and read and read, and I started practicing the teachings of the Scriptures. As I saw their fruit in my life, I came to the conclusion that the truth of the Scriptures was absolute. And if this was so, I knew I had to go all in: I had to believe either all of it or none of it. And so, with little more than a three-year-old faith and a blind trust in the truth of God's Word, I set to planning.

I examined our finances—the savings we had put away for a rainy day—and considered what I could bring in as a commercial fisherman on the river. By my calculations, between my savings and what I could make fishing the Ouachita, we had a three-year window for me to try and get a duck call business off the ground. That was enough for me. I knew God would come through and that he'd take care of Miss Kay and me if this dream was from him. But how would I convince Miss Kay?

Come to find out, it was easier than I thought it'd be. I told her the scheme and she agreed. That's all it took. We were off to the races.

Miss Kay found a good piece of land down by the river. It was prone to flooding, but while flooded timber is typically a real estate nightmare, it's a sportsman's dream. We sank our savings into that land and, after the 1976 school year, we moved into the small house on the property. I bought a commercial fishing license and, though I'd teach one more school year, I knew my direction.

By the summer of 1977, I'd quit teaching. From that point on I was full bore, all in on building my duck call business and fishing to make ends meet. In the early mornings I'd run the trotlines, hoop nets, and trammel nets up and down the Ouachita River. The banks of that river had once provided for Native Americans. It'd provided for the local rednecks too. Now it was providing for me and my family.

Morning after morning, setting those lines, I took comfort in the ways God provided for his creatures. The deer had a steady supply of acorns from the forest on either side of the river. Where the bottoms flattened out, a steady supply of wild millet, wild sunflowers, and sprangletop cropped up to feed the migrating ducks. The coyotes, beavers, wild foxes, and feral cats had everything they needed. What's more, the river rats, rednecks, and trappers—folks just like me—had all we needed to make ends meet. With new eyes to see the goodness of God, the words of Jesus came to mind: "Look at the birds of the air; they do not sow or reap or store away in barns, and yet your heavenly Father feeds them" (Matt. 6:26).

Those were the poorest years of my life, and some of my most labor intensive too. I fished, hunted, and trapped while the sun was up, and worked on my prototype duck calls in the meantime. But poor as we were, the absolute truth of God's Word stood. Not only had he rescued me from sin, shame, and certain death, but he was providing more than enough for my family's needs. In fact, on any given night, Miss Kay and I would host church folks of all shapes, sizes, and colors. Most of us were poor together, so they'd come with a pan of crackling bread or a pot of beans. We'd fry catfish from the river. We'd give thanks, break bread, and sing praises to the Lord for his goodness. Together we learned what it meant to share all things in common, just like the first church did in the book of Acts (2:44). Together we learned what the truth of the Scriptures meant—God really did provide for his faithful people.

Days and months passed, and I created my first duck call, which was whittled from scrap wood lying around my river home. I tested it on the river and discovered what I already believed to be true: I could command ducks with that call. Trouble was, without machinery, I couldn't produce the calls to scale. The other trouble was, without money, I couldn't procure machinery.

In *Happy, Happy, Happy*, I shared the story of taking my fellow church member and Howard Brothers executive Baxter Brasher duck hunting. I wrote of how he saw my prototype in use, how he said it was the best call he'd ever heard. I shared how he backed my enthusiasm and helped me procure a $25,000 loan to purchase the lathe I needed to ramp up production. Here's what I didn't share: Baxter agreed to help me because he'd been watching my life. He'd seen how committed I'd been to the Word of Truth that had saved me from death. He'd seen how I'd trusted the Lord's providence and took a leap of faith. He watched as Miss Kay and I shared all we had with whoever needed it. He'd been a keen observer. He said he'd found me to be a faithful student of our Master, and that he knew if I continued to live my life in the absolute truth of God's Word, if I continued to dedicate myself to the craft God had blessed me with, I'd do just fine.

Baxter was right. I reckon I've done just fine. I haven't missed a meal yet.

"God is dead," they said, trying to convince themselves it was true. And as they said it over and over again, they told themselves this too: *truth is dead, or at least relative.* In fact, that same *Time* article said just as much. In it the author wrote:

> Many of the theologians attempting to work out a new doctrine of God admit that they are uncertain as to the impact of their ultimate findings on other Christian truths; but they agree that such God-related issues as personal salvation in the afterlife and immortality will need considerable re-study.[1]

In other words, questioning the absolute truth of God's existence opens the door to all sorts of other questions too.

- If God is dead, what does he have to say? *Nothing.*
- If his word isn't true, what is the Bible but a good story and an ancient moral code? *Probably nothing.*
- If the Bible is nothing more than a good story, is there really an evil one himself? *It's doubtful.*
- If the Bible is only an ancient moral code, how can it apply today? *It probably doesn't.*
- If it doesn't apply, can there be a penalty for breaking that moral standard? Can there be a hell? *It's uncertain at best.*
- If there's no hell, why did Christ die? *Who knows, really? He was probably just a lunatic.*

This is the way it all breaks down, see. If the very existence of God is in question, then so are the absolute truths spoken by that God in the Bible. At best those truths are relative, they argue, and if all truth is relative, then aren't we free to chase our desires? What's keeping us from acting on every sexual impulse? Why not say what we want, drink what we want, take every advantage we can get? Why not abort babies, steal, murder? If there's no absolute standard for truth, who can say these things are wrong?

As I see it, there's only one problem with this line of thinking, and it's a big problem. It's all based on the lie that God is dead. A lie created by the deceiver himself, Satan.

Throughout the Bible the evil one has been known as a deceiver, a liar, and the lawless one. Jesus said he was a murderer and a liar from the beginning. As he said in the gospel of John, "When he lies, he speaks his native language, for he is a liar and the father of lies" (8:44). Paul told us that he comes disguised as an angel of light (2 Cor. 11:14). Maybe like one of those enlightened university professors, modern scientists, or politicians.

Though Satan has deceived men over and over again, Paul warned us of his schemes. He taught us exactly how the Devil and his end-time servant, the lawless one, operate. In his second letter to the Thessalonians, Paul wrote,

> The coming of the lawless one will be in accordance with how Satan works. He will use all sorts of displays of power through signs and wonders that serve the lie, and all the ways that wickedness deceives those who are perishing. They perish because they refused to love the truth and so be saved. For this reason God sends them a powerful delusion so that they will believe the lie and so that all will be condemned who have not believed the truth but have delighted in wickedness. (2:9–12)

Lies, lies, lies—they're the only weapon the evil one has in his arsenal. He uses those weapons against the human race, trying to deceive them so they'll turn away from God. So they'll forget his truths and chase their own desires down to death.

In the same way he warned the early church in Thessalonica, Paul also warned the Romans. He showed what happens when people fall for the lie that God is dead and fail to follow the absolute truth meant to lead them into light and life. He wrote,

> Furthermore, just as they did not think it worthwhile to retain the knowledge of God, so God gave them over to a depraved mind, so that they do what ought not to be done. They have become filled with every kind of wickedness, evil, greed and depravity. They are full of envy, murder, strife, deceit and malice. They are gossips, slanderers, God-haters, insolent, arrogant and boastful; they invent ways of doing evil; they disobey their parents; they have no understanding, no fidelity, no love, no mercy. Although they know God's righteous decree that those who do such things deserve death, they not only continue to do these very things but also approve of those who practice them. (1:28–32)

See? When God is dead, so is his divine truth. And without divine truth, without truth to govern our human conduct, we fall for the Devil's lie. Living in that lie, men and women become the worst versions of themselves.

It's true enough that godless men ignore the truth and find themselves in bondage to all manner of evil. But are they completely to blame? Not really. According to Scripture, they're not just following their own desires. They're filled by the very lying spirit himself. Paul wrote it plainly in his letter to the Ephesians:

> As for you, you were dead in your transgressions and sins, in which you used to live when you followed the ways of this world

and of the ruler of the kingdom of the air, the spirit who is now at work in those who are disobedient. (2:1–2)

See what's happening? It's the spirit of the evil one *in those* who are disobedient. I guess there's a kernel of truth to that old saying "The Devil made me do it."

We live in a dark day, a day when the Devil has indwelled so many and whispered, *All truth is relative.* He's convinced us there's no absolute moral standard for sexuality (which the Bible confines to the marital bed). There's no absolute truth regarding when life begins (which the Bible says begins before the first cells are knit in the womb). There's no absolute truth about the definition of marriage (which the Bible indicates as being between one man and one woman, till death do they part). There's no timeless and absolute truth about virtue, or law, or even what constitutes the church.

Everything is up in the air, the liar says, *so follow your own desires and make your own truth.*

Can there be any doubt that America has fallen under the delusion of the evil one? And yes, this is bad news. But here's the good news, the gospel news: Jesus came to show us the truth that would set us free from the evil one's delusions (John 8:32). Again, look at the writings of Paul:

Like the rest, we were by nature deserving of wrath. But because of his great love for us, God, who is rich in mercy, made us alive with Christ even when we were dead in transgressions—it is by grace you have been saved. And God raised us up with Christ and seated us with him in the heavenly realms in Christ Jesus, in order that in the coming ages he might show the incomparable riches of his grace, expressed in his kindness to us in Christ Jesus. (Eph. 2:3–7)

God saved us from evil. He saved us from wrath. He saved us because of his great love for us, and for what purpose? So that he could show us "the incomparable riches of his grace."

Sounds like a good deal if you ask me.

And once we're freed from sin and wrath, how do we live into those incomparable riches? We stake our lives on the absolute truth of the Bible.

What does the Bible say about the truth?

I'm glad you asked.

The Bible is God's written Word, and it contains his eternal, divine, and timeless truth. Repeatedly, King David, the man after God's own heart, recognized the truth of God's Word. In Psalm 25:5 (NKJV) he wrote, "Lead me in your truth and teach me, for you are the God of my salvation." Likewise, in Psalm 33:4 he wrote, "For the word of the LORD is right and true; he is faithful in all he does." Psalm 119:142, a psalm often attributed to David, reads, "Your righteousness is everlasting and your law is true."

Christ himself said there is objective and absolute truth. In fact, he went a step further. He claimed *he* was the absolute truth, saying, "I am the way and the truth and the life. No one comes to the Father except through me" (John 14:6). What was Jesus' message? There was no way to break free from the delusions of the enemy but to trust in his message and walk in his ways.

In his letter to the Ephesians, Paul wrote that the Gentiles were "darkened in their understanding and separated from the life of God because of the ignorance that is in them due to the hardening of their hearts" (4:18). They'd believed the lies of the Devil and engaged in "every kind of impurity, and they [were] full of greed" (v. 19). However, the Ephesian church had been taught a different way, the way of righteousness and holiness. Paul wrote,

> That, however, is not the way of life you learned when you heard about Christ and were taught in him in accordance with *the truth that is in Jesus.* You were taught, with regard to your former way of life, to put off your old self, which is being corrupted by its deceitful desires; to be made new in the attitude of your minds; and to put on the new self, created to be like God in true righteousness and holiness. (vv. 20–24, emphasis added)

The Bible promises that if we live according to his absolute truth and try our best to live sinless, godly lives, we'll enjoy the blessings of God. It also promises this: if we follow the truth, we'll be weird folks. John wrote it this way: "The reason the world does not know us is that it did not know him" (1 John 3:1). But if we remain faithful, we'll not only gain peace of mind and eternal life, we'll have the opportunity to influence some of our opponents. Why else would Paul instruct,

> Opponents must be gently instructed, in the hope that God will grant them repentance leading them to a knowledge of the truth,

and that they will come to their senses and escape from the trap of the devil, who has taken them captive to do his will. (2 Tim. 2:25–26)

Even those who've been indwelled by the evil one can be freed. I was.

We're two thousand years away from the incarnation of Christ, who had lived a morally perfect life of love, died as a sacrifice for our sins, and beat the grave so we, too, might beat it one day. We're two thousand years away from the writings of the apostles, the early followers of Christ who taught us to live like Christ, with lives of righteous, holy love. We're two thousand years away, but here's the thing about absolute truth: it doesn't change with time. It's as solid as petrified cypress. As immovable too.

So the world can claim that God has died and his truth has passed away with him. They can say all truth is relative, that it can be changed with the shifting desires of men. They can say I'm a crazy, uneducated, Bible-thumping river rat. They can say and say and say. You know what my response will be?

The truth ain't a buzzkill, dude. It'll give you life, peace of mind, and make you happy, happy, happy.

And just imagine it. If enough of my opponents—and there are plenty of them, to be sure—took hold of that truth, America might just have a shot. Think of how it'd impact American families, relationships, and standards of living. Wouldn't it reduce addiction, crime, drug use, and all our country's sicknesses? Wouldn't it make us a nation of harder workers and wiser managers of time and money? Wouldn't it give us a purpose beyond making money, working for the weekend, keeping up with the Joneses? I bet it'd lead to a more moral, just, and virtuous society too. It would cut down on sex scandals and race riots, I know that much. Wouldn't it give us eternal life?

Following the truth has its benefits, see.

From the moment I believed, I committed myself to the absolute truth of God's Word. I believed it all, even that he'd provide for me just like the Good Book says. And time after time, he's proved himself faithful to his Word.

Still, living into the truth ain't always easy. It wasn't all roses and daisies as I followed the path the Almighty laid out for me. There were times I wondered how he'd come through, times I thought Miss Kay and I might not make it. In fact, there were two separate occasions when I wondered whether God would keep his promises.

That initial loan left us strapped and, as I built Duck Commander, I sold everything but the house, Miss Kay, and the kids so I could make the payments. When the first loan renewal payment came due, Miss Kay and I didn't have the $600 we needed, an amount that wasn't chump change back in those days. Our bank account was down to four digits, including the two numbers after the decimal, and Miss Kay asked whether I'd need to get a job to make ends meet.

I recited the truths of the Bible, said that God would provide for us, his children. I told her we'd trust the Lord's promises. We'd believe all of it or none of it.

The days passed and I kept my eyes peeled. I figured he'd provide. I wondered whether I'd stumble upon a pot of money in the woods or whether I'd come into an inheritance. I didn't know, but I trusted.

On the day the loan was due, I awoke and made my way to the kitchen where Miss Kay was waiting. She asked how we'd make the loan payment, and I shot it to her straight, told her I wasn't sure.

"Let's just wait till the mail runs, and if nothing comes in, I'll march down to the bank and eat my crow," I said.

Secretly, I wondered whether I could find someone to lend me the money. Secretly, I feared the bank would take everything we had.

Around the noon hour, the mail lady pulled up and dropped off the day's mail. In it was a letter from the Bank of Tokyo. It was a certified check for $610, paid in advance for a shipment of calls to Japan. I handed the check to Miss Kay, and she looked at it, looked at me, then looked at the check again before bursting into tears. I told her she could take it to the bank and make the loan payment. She could keep the rest to buy something nice for herself, I said.

I'd relied on the promises of God, knew he'd provide according to his Word of truth, and I passed the first test. Six months later, I'd face that same test.

Another renewal payment was coming due, and knowing how close we'd cut it before, I decided I wouldn't wait for a last-minute miracle. Two weeks before the payment was due, I loaded up my john boat and started fishing the Ouachita hard. I ran the hoop nets and trotlines but caught little more than tin cans and rubber boots. Day after day I headed farther up the river, moving north into Sterlington, then farther north from there. Day after day, net after net, line after line, I came up empty. Every night on my slow trip back to the house, I prayed and asked God whether he'd come through. And every night I remembered the truth of Scriptures that God would provide for his children.

"Don't worry," I told Miss Kay. "I've staked my life on the truth of God's Word. It says he'll provide for his children. He will."

With a few days to spare before the loan came due, I ran back up the Ouachita and met up with some old farm boys. I explained my predicament and told them I'd need a haul of biblical proportions. They listened, then agreed to show me one of their honey holes just upriver. I cruised behind them, hoping those good ol' boys knew what they were doing, but when we cut the motors, I looked into the water of their fishing spot. Something wasn't right.

"It's too clear," I said. "We need to find some muddier water."

They stared back.

"Follow me, boys."

Thinking they might learn a thing or two from a commercial fisherman, they followed me back down to the Louisiana state line. I wasn't as familiar with this stretch, but on our way downriver, I spotted a promising run. There the Ouachita had overflowed the banks and stretched into the woods. There was a yellow, dingy patch of water that'd flooded an old timber road. I pointed to it and told the boys that was the spot.

"Get ready to see a miracle, boys," I said. "The Almighty is with me today. I can feel it."

We began to run the trot line over that flooded timber road, tying one end of the line to a tree, then running it on a diagonal to a tree on the other side. I'd decided to go for broke, decided to tie off a thousand hooks. I'd set them first, then go back and bait them. At least that was the plan. Before I got halfway through tying off the hooks, before I'd baited the first one, the line started jumping. Confused, the boys looked at me.

"Told you. The Almighty is here, boys."

We circled back to the first run and pulled up a hook. Attached to it was one of the largest eel catfish I'd ever caught. We worked the lines back and forth, and they never stopped jumping. Bewildered but amazed, the farm boys jumped in and started helping me take the fish off the line. We worked until the sun had almost set, and before it was over, my boat was riding low, almost sunk by the weight of the fish. I gave them a few bucks to help me load up the truck, and we said our goodbyes.

"Mark this date on your calendar, boys. You just witnessed a river rat miracle."

I drove the catch to market, and lo and behold, it was a miracle. My day's work weighed in at more than one thousand pounds, and the market handed me a note for $780, a note I took to the bank the next day. It allowed us to make the payment and put a little extra in the bank to invest in our young duck call company.

See? When we live in accordance with the Scriptures, when we trust in God, he provides.

The truth of God's Word is solid, unchanging, and sure. My life is a testament to it. I'd believed the truth of the Scriptures and went all in. The Bible said I could be freed from sin and shame, and it was true. The Bible said a moral and godly life would bring peace of mind, and it did. The Scriptures also said the Lord would bless and provide for his children who walk in the truth, and time after time, he did that too. Now, after years of believing and following this truth, I've seen firsthand the difference Christ can make in a life, a business, a television show, and ultimately, across a nation.

The way I see it, either I am the luckiest redneck in all of Northern Louisiana, or God blesses those who make an unwavering commitment to follow God's Word. And seeing as how my life was anything but lucky until I followed the truth, I reckon I know the truth.

America, this is where the rubber meets the road. You either believe in the absolute truth of the Bible, or you don't. You either repent and return to God's standard of living, or you continue to believe the lies of Satan and reap the heartache of evil. As for me and my house? We'll follow the truth, thank you very much, and if I had my way, America would test the promises of God and see that they are given to us in love. Americans would find the peace of mind, unity, and prosperity they so want.

THE LIE: GOD DID NOT CREATE LIFE.

THE TRUTH: GOD IS THE AUTHOR OF LIFE AND ONLY HE CAN NOURISH AND SUSTAIN IT.

In my college years, I ran up on some enlightened professors who were firmly convinced we'd killed God. There was no need for him anymore, they said, probably never was. They taught us that men were not the product of a creating God, but instead, we'd evolved from apes some millions of years ago. Where did the apes come from? Good question, they said. The apes evolved from fish, which had grown legs and crawled from the salt water onto the land. Where'd the fish come from? They'd evolved from single cells, had doubled up and grown tails. Where'd the single cells come from? They'd been swimming around in the salt water since just after the big bang, the professors said.

Huh?

I didn't ever believe the lie that men had evolved from apes, or fish, or single cells that crawled out of the salt water. I was a man of the woods, and I'd never seen a catfish crawl out of the mud and turn into an ape. And sure, I hadn't been around for millions of years, but common sense is common sense. Nope, I didn't really believe in evolution at all. But until I came to know the power of Jesus in my life, I didn't stop to consider the simplest question: Where had all this life come from?

After running up on Jesus, I'd found the peace of mind I so wanted. And as I came to understand the absolute truth of his Word, as I ate the Scriptures day after day, I found that the Almighty really was the source of the fullest life. In Genesis I read how God created the heavens and earth, how he started with light, then created fish, plants, and animals before making man. I read the gospel of John and through it discovered that the creative process had occurred through Jesus himself. "Through him all things were made; without him nothing was made that has been made," John wrote (John 1:3). I read the words of Paul to the Colossians, too, read how "in him all things were created: things in heaven and on earth, visible and invisible, whether thrones or powers or rulers or authorities; all things have been created through him and for him" (1:16).

Not only had Christ been the creating agent of all life; he'd also come to bring life where the enemy of our souls had tried to bring death. Jesus put it plainly in the book of John: "The thief comes only to steal and kill and destroy; I have come that they may have life, and have it to the full" (10:10). He didn't just say it, though. As the Author and Sustainer of all life, he backed up his words as he walked among the people. He raised a dead man, Lazarus, to new life (John 11:38–44). He raised Jairus's daughter from death to life (Mark 5:21–43). He even took five loaves of bread and two fish and multiplied it to feed more than five thousand people (Matt. 14:13–21). That act of creating food for so many hungry people— bread and fish—wasn't that a life-giving act? And this is nothing to say of the fact that Jesus came to free us from eternal death and raise us to everlasting life.

The Scriptures couldn't be clearer. The Almighty is the Author and Sustainer of true life, and he works his purposes out through Jesus Christ.

As I grew in the truth of the Scriptures, I began to examine the life-giving ways of Christ in the world around me. Still waiting for my duck call business to take off, I was living off the land to make ends meet. As I worked, I brought my boys alongside me and taught them to notice God's creative, life-giving genius. Everything that was created, I told them, was created by him for our good. He created all this for our good, to sustain our life.

On some occasions after the morning chores, the boys and I would sit on the game trails and watch the animals. We'd watch raccoons and foxes. We'd see the occasional snake crossing the path. We'd watch the deer come to feed on the acorns that fell on the trail. When the deer moved on, we'd walk over to the spot just under one of those mighty oaks, and I'd pick up one of those acorns and pass it over to Willie or Jason or Al. I'd ask them to roll it around in their fingers, to feel how small and light it was. I'd point them to the massive oak tree rising over the trail. That tree, I'd tell them, took a couple of hundred years to grow, and mature as it was, it could produce more than twenty tons of timber. It could be felled, sawed into planks, turned into a kitchen table, a full set of chairs, and frame for the house, and there'd still be a good bit of timber left over. All that wood, all of it used to sustain so much life, and it came from a single seed that weighed only an ounce or two.

Wasn't the Almighty creative?

Of course we harvested our fair share of game, mostly ducks

and deer, and I taught the boys how the Almighty gave us land to support game, which in turn supported us. He'd given us the best game trails for deer. He'd also blessed us with the perfect feeding ground for the overwintering ducks. Our fields were flecked with wild grasses, sedges, and millets, and when the weather turned, when their nesting grounds in Canada were frozen over and un-inhabitable, the ducks would come to our neck of the woods for a more hospitable habitat. They'd fly to our fields, flooded in the winter, and take advantage of the feed. We'd be waiting for them there in our floating duck blinds, ones built on top of the trunks of fallen cypress logs that the Almighty had filled with a rot-resistant resin. We'd call them with our Duck Commander duck calls (also made from wood provided by the Almighty), then we'd stand up in the blinds and take advantage of the perfect shooting lanes. It was almost as if the Almighty had designed all of this just for us, just to sustain our lives through the duck harvest. And what'd we do with those birds?

- Duck gumbo
- Duck jambalaya
- Roasted duck
- Duck and dressing

But it wasn't just ducks. I showed my boys how the Almighty provided littler things to sustain us, too, things like crawfish and muscadines and mayhaws. I taught them how to turn those crawfish into the best étouffée, and Miss Kay showed them how the wild mayhaws—a fruit the Almighty saw fit to bestow upon Louisiana—could be turned into the world's best jelly. Life was all around us, I taught them, and God was its Author. It was almost as if he knew what his creation would need to have a full life. It was almost as if he pulled it all together for our support, sustenance, and nourishment.

Those were the days before monetary success, and the life we lived was simple. We didn't have computers or cell phones (I still don't), and I wasn't constantly distracted by business figures, by profits and losses. We weren't distracted by the twenty-four-hour news cycles either. The Robertson family wasn't driven by money or greed, and we didn't chase after the newest house or the shiniest car. We didn't live a decadent life by any stretch of the imagination, but still our life was full. Why? We understood we were not just the product of random chance, of some cluster of cells climbing out of the salt water. No, sir. We knew the truth: Jesus, the Author and Creator of life, filled it all. Knowing that truth, we didn't worry about where our next meal came from or how we'd make ends meet. We trusted the Almighty, and year after year his provision arrangement worked out just fine for us.

From America's inception, our Founding Fathers recognized the God of the Bible as the Author and Sustainer of life. As I'll show later in this book, they trusted the absolute truth of his Scriptures so much that they created a system of laws based on its principles. Likewise, many states did the same. Some states, like Tennessee, enacted legislation that prohibited public school teachers from teaching Darwinian evolution or anything other than the biblical account of creation. Theories of evolution were outlawed, and teachers were tried and convicted for violating the law. In fact, it was this law that led to the famous Scopes trial in the 1920s, the trial that resulted in ACLU-backed John Scopes being found guilty for teaching evolution.[1]

The Tennessee law would stay on the books until 1967, when the Tennessee legislature repealed it. To this day the religion of evolution can be taught in Tennessee, and it all started with the move to kill God in the late 1960s. The sixties—what an era.

When America took to kill'n God, they aborted any notion that life was divinely inspired by him. The enemy of God's creation, the liar and murderer from the beginning, came and whispered the insidious question, *If there is no God, how could he be the Author of life?* It was a lie that took hold in the American consciousness, one that led to our institutions of higher learning teaching wild theories of evolution. But it was also the lie that led America to reexamine the divine inspiration of life from conception. It's the lie that led the United States Supreme Court to allow abortions in the 1971 opinion of Roe v. Wade, a decision that's led to the abortion of more than sixty million babies according to some estimates.[2] In my view, it's the lie that's led to epic proportions of violent crime too. Gang violence, mass shootings, murder, and rape—if God isn't the Author of life, if all of life is just chance and happenstance, who's to keep us from taking it?

Should it surprise us that the lie of the enemy would lead us to so much violence and murder? After all, as Jesus said, the Devil was a liar and murderer from the beginning.

As if abortion and violent crime aren't bad enough—and they are bad enough—kill'n God has led some folks to other asinine positions. As a hunter, a royal pain in the behind of animal treatment groups like PETA, I've heard all the arguments against harvesting wild game. They claim that all life is the same, all climbed out of the same saltwater pond. So, they ask, what gives man the right to take the life of a duck or deer?

God and my opposable thumbs, I say.

The truth is, God is the Author of all life—human, animal, plant. And as if to remove any question, the entire Bible starts with this sentence: "In the beginning God created the heavens and the earth" (Gen. 1:1). But he didn't just create life. He also organized it all for the benefit of his greatest creation: mankind. The Genesis account seems to make this plain too. After making a beautiful garden, God placed man and woman in it and then gave them a simple task: be fruitful, multiply, and fill the earth. But how would man get what he needed to be fruitful and multiply? How would his needs be met? God thought that through. All that other life the Almighty had created? He'd allow men to use it to sustain their own lives. The writer of Genesis recorded it this way:

Then God said, "Let Us make man in Our image, according to Our likeness; let them have dominion over the fish of the sea, over the birds of the air, and over the cattle, over all the earth and over every creeping thing that creeps on the earth." (Gen. 1:26 NKJV)

Just chapters later, after God brought Noah and his family through the Flood, he gave a similar command to Noah:

"Be fruitful and increase in number and fill the earth. The fear and dread of you will fall on all the beasts of the earth, and on all the birds in the sky, on every creature that moves along the ground, and on all the fish in the sea; they are given into your hands. Everything that lives and moves about will be food for you. Just as I gave you the green plants, I now give you everything." (9:1–3)

God gave us everything we needed to sustain our lives. Plant life for wood and construction materials, animal life for food and fur—God allows us to use those things for our benefit.

The question remains: What is the purpose of all this life the Almighty created for us? Why did he give us plants and animals to subdue for our own provision? The answer is simple: God wanted us to understand his goodness. In his sermon before the Areopagus, recorded in the book of Acts, Paul put it this way:

[H]e himself gives everyone life and breath and everything else.
. . . God did this so that they would seek him and perhaps reach

out for him and find him, though he is not far from any one of us. (17:25, 27)

God wanted us to see the ways he created life to feed us, nourish us, and help us flourish, and through that, he wanted us to know just how much he loves us. He left us a game trail straight to his character. As Paul would later write to the Romans, God wanted his love for us to be "understood from what has been made, so that people are without excuse" (1:20).

It's pretty simple, really. God, the Author of life, created the perfect conditions to sustain man. He created mankind to be the highest of earthly life (just "a little lower than the angels," the writer of Hebrews wrote), and he gave us plants to cultivate, to use for food and shelter. He gave us animals to harvest for food and clothing. The Author of life had a pretty good plan: create life to sustain life. And when we remember nature's purpose, when we remember the truth of its sustaining force, it should always and ever point us back to the goodness of the Almighty. It should remind us of how much he cares for and loves us.

Yes, plant and animal life were given to mankind for our good. But there remained one variety of life mankind was not allowed to harm—another human life. Why? After instructing Noah and his family that it was permissible to take the life of an animal for food, the Almighty said, "Whoever sheds man's blood, by man his blood shall be shed, for in the image of God He made man" (Gen. 9:6 NKJV). See? Murderers open themselves to the potential of murder. It's part of the cosmic order. Why? God made us in his own image, distinct from the animals, and killing another human destroys that image. And that begs the question: When do humans take on that image of God? Probably just as soon as blood is involved, which, the best I can tell, is when a baby is first formed in the mother's womb (Ps. 139:13).

The enemy came and he convinced us that God is not the Author of life, that all of it happened by chance. He's convinced us that we aren't made in God's image, but that we've evolved from monkeys. He's made us believe that our unborn babies aren't really alive, that they're nothing but clumps of tissue to be disposed of. The evil one has blinded us to God's creating and sustaining ways, and what's the result? We protect animals and kill babies. We've turned to murder and mayhem. We lack the peace and presence of God that comes from understanding God's life-authoring ways. I've noticed this lack of peace as America seems to be spinning ever out of control. Have you?

Liberal after liberal—vegans, card-carrying PETA members, and the like—accuse me of cowardice for hunting. They say I'm evil or cruel for taking the life of an animal, a coward for calling the poor little duckies to the slaughter. But I don't take the life of any animal—duck, deer, whatever—lightly. When I dispatch a duck—and I've dispatched my fair share—I do it for one reason only. What's that reason? It's a biblical one. As God told Peter in the book of Acts, "Get up, Peter. Kill and eat" (10:13). And when I do, I'm thankful to the Almighty for using life to sustain my life.

I only kill when authorized by the Scriptures—wild game for nourishment. In modern America, though, those same folks who won't kill animals kill unborn babies. They call it being pro-choice, though they give no thought to the choice of whether the unborn baby wants to live or die. And every time another unborn baby is aborted, they shake their fists at God himself, telling him, "You're not the author of *this* life."

It's not just abortion either. Elsewhere in America, men kill other men for sport.

During the writing of this book, I've seen an uptick in the violence, an unprecedented epidemic of mass murder on American soil. In fact, on the morning I outlined this very chapter, I awoke to the news that some maniac, a man under the influence of the evil one, rented a room in a Las Vegas high-rise hotel overlooking a country music venue. He smuggled an armory's worth of weaponry into that hotel room, and when the guitars started playing, he opened a window and took aim at the crowd below. It was his makeshift blind, and he took full advantage of it. Ripping off round after round, he cut down the folks at the concert like they were less than animals.

The shooter was neutralized by the police officers, which is the media's way of saying he was dispatched with deadly force. When the smoke cleared, when the bodies were counted, he'd murdered fifty-eight people in cold blood, and another 489 were wounded. The folks on the news were confounded. How could such a thing happen in America?

Really, Mr. News Dude?

That Las Vegas shooting was just the beginning. Thirty-five days later another man under the influence of the evil one entered the First Baptist Church of Sutherland Springs, Texas, on a Sunday morning, and he opened fire. When the shooting stopped, twenty-six were dead. Among those twenty-six were women and children, including several elderly and handicapped people.

And that gunman? He would've slaughtered more if a selfless and well-armed American, Stephen Willeford, hadn't put himself in harm's way. Hearing the shots from his home, he loaded his gun and ran to the church barefooted. There, he saw the gunman and exchanged gunfire with him. One of those bullets pierced the madman's body armor and drove him back to his vehicle, in which he sped away. Willeford and another townsman gave chase and followed the gunman to the place where he eventually took his own life. Why would Willeford charge into the heart of violence? What gave him the courage to put an end to a mass murderer's reign of terror? According to his attorney, Willeford believed God—the Author of life—used him as a tool to stop evil. See the impact a man can have when he's armed with the truth and a gun?

Two mass murders in just over a month, both of which occurred while I worked on this very book. And guess what? There will likely be another mass shooting before this book heads to print. There may be a few more between the date this book is printed and the date you start reading it. There may be yet another before you pass it on to your neighbor.

Death, chaos, and mass murder. It's a slaughterhouse out there, a real meat grinder, and is it any wonder? If we've killed God, why not kill a man or two? If we've killed God, what are the consequences for our acts of murder?

And they call me crazy for killing ducks?

The liberal politicians, university professors, and talking heads on the news offer different reasons for the uptick in these kinds of mass murders. They point to study after study and pin the blame on the gun industry. They talk about mental health issues. And though they are well meaning, these folks fail to recognize the true root of the problem: men do not respect the image of God in their fellow man. Why? They don't believe God created man in the first place. Having taken God out of the equation, having failed to retain the knowledge of God, the wicked men of America have been given over to their depraved minds. They've become just like their father, the evil one—a liar and murderer from the beginning.

I've retained the truth of God's Word and know that he has authored all life for my benefit and sustenance. I know all life the Almighty created—plants, animals, and my fellow man—points me always to God's invisible qualities, his care, love, and protection. And by reading the Scriptures, I know that Jesus Christ is the ultimate embodiment of that life, that he came to show us how to live it to the full. He came to free us from eternal death and bring us to eternal life too. It's that truth that anchors my soul and brings me great peace.

Life—see? It's a gift from God.

From time to time good folks ask me how we might decrease abortion or gang violence or mass shooting. They ask if we should change abortion laws or whether we should create stricter gun legislation. They ask whether government policies can make a difference. I tell them I don't know, but I doubt it. I don't reckon any amount of legislation can change the hearts of those under the influence of the evil one. There is an antidote, though, and it's simple.

America, return to the truth.

How?

Remember God, the Author of life, and see how he's created all life to nourish and sustain us. As you remember, partner with the Almighty in tending to life. Leave the slaughterhouse and get out to nature. Cultivate and harvest a little. See how tender the life he's created is, how tasty it is too. And as you see the beauty of God in his nature, recognize the beauty in the life of your fellow man also. See how he was created in the image of God. Remember that his blood ain't yours to take, whether the blood of an unborn baby or elderly woman minding her business in a Texas church. Return to the truth. Choose life. And when you do, watch as God saves your soul. And then give thanks.

THE LIE: SEX IS FOR SELF-GRATIFICATION.

THE TRUTH: GOD CREATED SEXUALITY FOR HIS PURPOSES AND OUR GOOD.

I grew up in a humble home, one that didn't have a bathtub, running water, or a commode. We lived in a simple log home with board floors, and we tended to our business in a dirt-floored outhouse. We had a milk cow, a garden, and a few hogs we raised to slaughter. When we weren't tending to livestock or the garden, we were hunting or fishing for our food. We were industrious, hardworking, and had little time to run around. We were anything but free.

Times were tight, and even though we didn't have a lot of capital in those days, my mother and father raised us to value some things more than money. We were raised to do right, to live moral lives, and to value integrity.

As I said in the opening chapters of this book, I never quite understood the truth of the gospel. I missed it for so many years. But that doesn't mean that my parents weren't godly in their own ways. My mother was kind, generous, and hospitable. She didn't make distinctions among people based upon money, class, or color. My dad was a stoic, hardworking roughneck who spent a great deal of time outside the home working in the oil fields. When he was home from the oil fields, he'd make sure we attended Sunday church services, and though the truth of the gospel escaped me, I knew a few things for certain: good Christians didn't drink, do drugs, or have sex before marriage.

My folks reinforced the moral messages of their church and made sure we knew there'd be consequences if my brother or I took to partying. The truth was, with all the work ol' Si and I had to do to help make ends meet, we didn't have much time to raise a ruckus. Our opportunities to get blitzed, high, or chase tail were regulated by church, family, and work.

I ran up on Miss Kay while I was still living under my parents' strict moral code. I was sixteen, and she was two years my junior, and I knew from the start that she was the one for me. We took to each other like ducks to water—analogy intended—and whenever I had any free time, I spent it with Miss Kay. We dated through our high school years, and just before college, we were married and had our first son, Alan. But as I began to enjoy success on the football field at Louisiana Tech, I started partying more and more with my teammates, often without Miss Kay, who was too busy rearing little Al. The partying gave me a taste of freedom, a taste of what it meant to chase my own desires like a Labrador puppy might chase its own tail.

Come to find out, if you chase your tail long enough, you'll catch it.

For the next several years, I spiraled down into my own desires, into booze and pills and easy women. The hippie movement was on, and though I was no hippie, I enjoyed the fruits of their sexual revolution, all the while leaving Miss Kay at home to tend to the children by herself. By the time Miss Kay left me, I'm sorry to say I was a regular whoremonger. And without Miss Kay to stand in the way of my sexual appetite, I did what I wanted, with whom I wanted, and I did it all in the name of freedom. All that sex wasn't freedom at all, though. It didn't satisfy my itch for long, and only left me with guilt, shame, and a suffocating loneliness. It was, of course, that guilt, shame, and loneliness that drove me back to the arms of Miss Kay, and ultimately into the arms of the Almighty.

Guilt and shame have their purpose, see.

When I heard the good news of Jesus, when I realized he'd freed me from all my sins and given me a new life, both now and in eternity, everything changed. In that change, some things didn't need to be explained by the preacher. I knew my days of law breaking were over. I knew my days of drinking and getting high had come to an end. I knew it was time to rededicate myself to God-honoring work, to building something that would provide for my family, church, and community. More than anything, though, I knew my personal sexual revolution was over. I was finished running around on Miss Kay.

I dedicated myself to the truth of the Scriptures and learned there really were moral absolutes. Time and time again, the Scriptures warned against the kind of sexual immorality that had so marked my life. As I learned to walk in the light of God's Word instead of the darkness of my own desire, I found I was making an easy trade. Sexual purity and dedication to Miss Kay were more satisfying than all the sexual freedom in the world. Almost fifty years later, I can tell you this: I haven't missed those days of debauchery for a minute.

There are things in life that seem self-explanatory, things you shouldn't need a preacher to tell you. We should all do good. We should love our neighbors. We should work hard, be industrious and honorable. No man should run around on his wife. Aren't these things just common sense?

One would think.

But if there's anything the Scriptures teach, it's this: when we ignore the God of the universe and chase our own desires, we fall under the delusions of the evil one. What should be evident isn't. Common sense seems illogical. And in this delusion we become blind to the truth of God. This, I reckon, is why the writers of the New Testament wrote about sexuality with regularity.

There's no mystery about sex and sexuality in the Bible. In the Genesis account we read that God created Adam and Eve—male and female he created them—and he told them to "be fruitful and increase in number; fill the earth and subdue it" (1:28). God made us to procreate, to fill the world with humans who'd manage his resources—resources like grain, Arkansas traveler tomatoes, and best of all, ducks. To facilitate this procreation he gave us a gift— sex. That gift was meant to be shared by one man and one woman, and the best I can tell, it was God's original intent that the two would share this gift exclusively within the bonds of their marital union.

It's not just the Genesis account, though, that shows that God's design for sex is within the confines of marriage. Throughout the books of Old Testament law, God shows time and time again how his intent is for sex to be celebrated in marriage. Solomon, one of the wisest men in all of the Scriptures, wrote an entire book about sexuality, showing how it's a gift meant to be shared in marriage, and in the Proverbs he was more explicit about restraining sexual desire, writing:

> May your fountain be blessed,
>> and may you rejoice in the wife of your youth.
> A loving doe, a graceful deer . . .
>> may you ever be intoxicated with her love.
> Why, my son, be intoxicated with another man's wife?
>> Why embrace the bosom of a wayward woman?
>
> (5:18–20)

The New Testament is not silent on the matter either. Throughout the writings to the early church, the apostles gave clear instruction on sex and sexuality. In the earliest days of the church, the truth of Jesus spread to the Gentiles—the hippies, rednecks, and river rats of their day. As it did, a question arose in the Jewish church about whether these new converts should be circumcised and whether they'd need to abide by the law of Moses. A council was convened to discuss the issue, and Peter spoke his mind on the matter. They'd been given the Holy Spirit as a sign of their acceptance even though they hadn't learned the law of Moses, he said. So why should these new church members be saddled with all the rules of the law? Instead, they should abide by only four rules: "abstain from food sacrificed to idols, from blood, from the meat of strangled animals and from sexual immorality" (Acts 15:29).

Among the simplest truths shared with the first church was this: keep your sex in the right place.

Sure, you say, but what exactly does it mean to avoid sexual immorality? How do you keep your sex in the right place? As if to remove all doubt, Paul addressed this issue in his letter to the Corinthian church, writing, "Each man should have sexual relations *with his own wife*, and each woman *with her own husband*. The husband should fulfill his marital duty to his wife, and likewise the wife to her husband" (1 Cor. 7:2–3, emphasis added). To the Hebrews the epistle writer penned a similar instruction: "Marriage should be honored by all, and the marriage bed kept pure, for God will judge the adulterer and all the sexually immoral" (Heb. 13:4).

It doesn't take a brain surgeon to sort out the Scriptures. This ain't rocket science. The instruction of the Scriptures is clear. Sex was made for marriage, for one man and one woman to share within the confines of marriage.

Time and time again, Paul reiterated his teachings to the Gentiles about sexual purity and warned them against sexual immorality. In his first letter to the Thessalonians, he wrote,

It is God's will that you should be sanctified: that you should avoid sexual immorality; that each of you should learn to control your own body in a way that is holy and honorable, not in passionate lust like the pagans, who do not know God; and that in this matter no one should wrong or take advantage of a brother or sister. The Lord will punish all those who commit such sins, as we told you and warned you before. For God did not call us to be impure, but to live a holy life. Therefore, anyone who rejects this instruction does not reject a human being but God, the very God who gives you his Holy Spirit. (4:3–8)

Again, in his letter to the Ephesians, he wrote, "Among you there must not be even a hint of sexual immorality . . . because these are improper for God's holy people" (5:3).

What happens, though, when mankind exchanges the truth of God for the lies of the enemy? What happens when they believe that they've killed God, that they've freed themselves from his reign and rule? In his letter to the Romans, Paul answered this question, writing that when people suppress the truth of God, he "[gives] them over in the sinful desires of their hearts to sexual impurity for the degrading of their bodies with one another" (1:24). And what is the result?

Hold on, America; this is where the Scriptures get unpopular.

Believing the lie of the enemy and falling into a deep delusion,

Even their women exchanged natural sexual relations for unnatural ones. In the same way the men also abandoned natural relations with women and were inflamed with lust for one another. Men committed shameful acts with other men, and received in themselves the due penalty for their error. (Rom. 1:26–27)

Sexual immorality, sexual gratification with whomever, wherever—these are signs of a people under the influence of the enemy's lies. And as Paul promises, folks under this delusion will receive their penalty. What is that due penalty?

The Bible isn't silent about the bodily penalties to be paid for sexual immorality. In his first letter to the Corinthians, Paul referenced the story of the Israelites' forty-year journey through the wilderness, and how some were seduced by the Moabite women. The Lord's anger burned against them, the Bible says, and some sort of plague ravaged the people (Num. 25:1–9). Of the story, Paul wrote, "We should not commit sexual immorality, as some of them did—and in one day twenty-three thousand of them died" (10:8).

Twenty-three thousand Israelites died from a plague that struck because of their sexual immorality? Sounds familiar, maybe like the sexually transmitted disease epidemic of today? I suppose I'll take heat for implying the Almighty uses STDs as a measure of judgment against those who ignore his laws, but I'm just telling you what the Bible says. I report; you decide.

Even if sickness, disease, and potential death were not a consequence of sexual immorality in this life, the eternal penalty should inspire us to obey God's standards for sexual purity. What is that penalty? It's the ultimate punishment, the kind that transcends time and space. As the writers of the New Testament wrote on multiple occasions, the sexually immoral will not inherit the kingdom of God (1 Cor. 6:9; Eph. 5:3; Heb. 12:15–17; Jude v. 7). The book of Revelation puts it this way: "The cowardly, the unbelieving, the vile, the murderers, the sexually immoral, those who practice magic arts, the idolaters and all liars—they will be consigned to the fiery lake of burning sulfur. This is the second death" (Rev. 21:8).

You can make your own decision, but as for me, I'd rather be led to the quiet streams of the Twenty-third Psalm—the streams where Miss Kay makes our bed—than be cast into the fiery lake of sulfur. But hey, to each his own.

On a morning like any other, I worked the river bottoms. I tended to the food regime, made sure there was plenty of wild millet, sprangle-top, smartweed, and sedges growing in the field so the ducks would have enough feed come winter. I cut down undesirables and pulled out the chicken spike, a weed that chokes out plants the ducks use for feed. I cleaned the brush around the blinds and cut back a few trees that'd grown in the field where the ducks would land when the fields flooded. I spent some time on the back roads that connected our hunting lands too. There I spotted a feral cat on the hunt and saw a cottonmouth crossing toward the levee. It was a day of simple admiration for God's creation, and I worked in it, gave thanks for it, and offered a few simple prayers along the way. This is the sort of peaceful life granted to a man who isn't always on the prowl chasing down his every animal instinct.

Morning gave way to noon, and I made my way back to the house. I hung my gun on the stand next to my recliner, kicked back, and flipped on the news while Miss Kay brought me my lunch. The news anchor was discussing some dude out of Hollywood, California, a fella named Harvey Weinstein. He was a big shot movie producer, the woman said, a well-resourced man with a great deal of influence in the entertainment industry. It was said Weinstein had used his big-shot status to coerce women into having sex with him, and the story went on to detail the ways he threatened women to keep them quiet. According to the reports, Weinstein, one of the kingpins of Hollywood, couldn't keep his pants zipped, and now he'd been ousted from his company, and who knew what other ramifications there might be.

I picked up a few potato chips and thought about it. Who'da thunk some Hollywood fat cat, a producer in one of the most sexually permissive industries in all of America, would have used his influence to prey on women? I would have.

Day gave way to day, and in the weeks that followed, sexually abused women began coming out of the woodwork. They outed man after man who they said had sexually abused them, and it seemed I couldn't turn on the news without hearing a new story of sexual harassment. A Democratic senator from Minnesota was accused of sexually harassing a former Playboy model on a USO tour to Kuwait. Roy Moore, the former judge and Republican hopeful for the Senate, a man I'd spoken on behalf of in the electoral primaries, was accused of sexual misconduct with more than one underage girl. A morning talk show anchor from a major network found himself in a sex scandal. Those were just a few of the ones whose alleged sexual immorality made the news.

Liberals, conservatives, atheists, Christians—they've all found their way into the news cycle these days, all been accused of using their power to force their way into the pants of women. Why? They forgot, ignored, or never knew the truth of God's Word. They apparently exchanged the truth about God's design for sex for the lie that sex is all about self-gratification, and following this lie has led them to their end. They've suffered embarrassment, shame, and in some cases loss of career and capital. And that's not to say anything of the penalties that might not be so evident.

What kind of penalties?

Consider this statement from the Centers for Disease Control and Prevention (CDC) website: "STDs are a substantial health challenge facing the United States." Nothing could be truer. Look at the statistics. As of the writing of this book, both the CDC and the mainstream media estimate that somewhere around 110 million Americans have a sexually transmitted disease (STD), and this number isn't a stagnant number. It's increasing. In fact, as of 2016, the CDC estimates that nearly twenty million new sexually transmitted infections occur every year.[1] More than two million cases of the three nationally tracked and reported STDs—chlamydia, gonorrhea, and syphilis—were reported in the United States in 2016, the highest number ever.[2] As stated by the mainstream media rag, the *New York Times*, "The incidence of chlamydia, gonorrhea and syphilis is increasing." (The epidemic is so bad, see, even the *Times* doesn't try to spin the truth.) Syphilis—a disease nearly eradicated a decade ago—rose 18 percent from 2015 to 2016 (9 cases per 100,000 people).[3]

What's the result of this increase in diseases? Debilitating illness and resulting death that leads to "almost $16 billion in health care costs annually."[4] Think the people of this good country could use $16 billion? Sho' nuff.

The truth of the Scriptures has played out in modern-day America. We've done our best to kill God, so is it any wonder we've believed the Devil's lie and followed him into an age of sexual promiscuity? Is it any wonder we're being consumed by our own lusts? Is it any wonder that infidelity runs rampant in our country, that marriages are falling apart at the rate of nearly 50 percent? Should it shock us that men—both Christian and non-Christian alike—struggle with online pornography addictions? Should it surprise us that one of the most godless, sexually permissive industries—the movie industry—based in Hollywood, California, has produced no shortage of sexual predators? (Hollywood, California? Surprise, surprise, surprise.) Should we be shocked that prostitution rings, infidelity, and sexual harassment have been uncovered in Washington, DC, the seat of a government that's done it's best to kill God? Nope. As we say down here on the river bottoms, the sins born in America's sexual revolution have come home to roost. The revenge of the hippies is upon us.

Make no mistake; God's Word is true. Sexual immorality comes with a price, a penalty. And if we don't turn back to the truth of God's Word, our society will continue to suffer both here and in the next life. There's a remedy, though, a remedy that might cure the ills that plague so many in our country. It's a remedy that flows from simple river-rat logic: save your sex for marriage; be disease free; marry a disease-free spouse; keep your sex within the confines of that marriage. The result?

No more unwanted pregnancies. Zero.

No more STDs. Zippo.

No more sexual harassment cases. None. Sounds like a deal.

Of course, I've preached this message for a good many years now, since before I made my first dollar on a duck call. I continued to preach it as Duck Commander grew into a million-dollar corporation and as Miss Kay and I became household names through *Duck Dynasty*. And as I travel and speak more and more, I've protected my commitment to sexual purity by carrying two things with me everywhere I go: my Bible—the Word of Truth—and Miss Kay. And guess what—I've not been involved in any sexual scandals, haven't been accused of sexually harassing a woman, and haven't spent the first dollar on treatment for a sexually transmitted disease.

Feasting on the Scriptures and committing to my wife—see? This is what it means to have safe sex. This is what it means to keep your sex safe.

Not everyone appreciates this commitment; that's true enough. It's no secret that I've taken fire over my beliefs, as some have accused me of homophobia and hatred for reporting what the Scriptures say. But let me say it straight—I don't hate anyone who's mired in what the Bible calls sin. In fact, I love them. If I truly hated them, I wouldn't share the truth with them. I wouldn't use every platform at my disposal to tell them of the saving work of Jesus, to offer them freedom from all their guilt and shame, and to give them an opportunity to live in eternal glory.

So, do I sit in judgment over America's sexual immorality? Nah. For starters, why should I judge? I haven't lived a sexually perfect life. What's more, it ain't my job to judge. That kind of judgment belongs to the Almighty. And anyway, sitting in judgment is about as useful as cursing the fields for not producing enough millet or smartweed in any given season. Instead of cursing the fields when the food supply runs low, I get to work. I disk the field, plant some millet, and wait for the Almighty to do his thing. And guess what, American Christian? It's time to sow some good spiritual seed, especially as it relates to sexual perversion and immorality. How? I'm glad you asked.

Declare the good and absolute truth of God's Word as it relates to sexuality, even if you've had your own indiscretions. Share the standards of godliness he gave us for our good. Show how a commitment to sexual purity within the confines of marriage—one man, one woman, both disease-free—can save folks from heartache, guilt, and shame. Show how it might save our society, too, how it might save us from broken marriages, financial ruin, and so much disease and death. Remind the people in your own communities that a commitment to sexual purity is a commitment to the truth. And don't keep this news from the sexual harassers, perverts, and cheaters. Go to them in love and offer the free gift of Christ to them; offer them deliverance from all their sin and shame.

Yes, the truth of the Bible is like millet, and the people of God should sow it everywhere we go. Sow it in the hopes that the Almighty will turn his favor toward us, that he'll bring us healing and wholeness. Sow it in the hopes that we'll reap the rewards of that harvest. The Word of God—it's the ultimate food supply.

America—wake up, oh sleeper! It's time to return to the truth. Sex was created by God for our pleasure and his purpose, but it needs to be kept in the right place. If you've not lived in that truth, though, repent. Return to the truth. Find your eternal freedom from sin and shame, and gain the gift of life eternal. In his great love God offers it to everyone. Even Harvey Weinstein.

6

THE LIE: VIRTUE IS OUTDATED.

THE TRUTH: GOD'S STANDARD FOR ALL
TIME IS THE STANDARD OF VIRTUE.

had mended fences with Miss Kay, had begun sharing the absolute truth of God's words with my old running buddies, and was building a growing duck call business. I did my best to apply biblical principles in my workplace—work hard, don't lie, don't cheat, don't overspend—and those principles were paying off. This isn't to say we were wealthy. By every worldly standard, we were still poor. All in all, though, we had everything we needed.

There was no arguing the fruit of a virtuous life, and as I grew into my role as a father, I wanted to teach these virtues to my boys. I wanted them to develop good character so they might walk in the blessings of the Almighty. So I did what any other godly river rat with a commercial fishing license might do. I put my boys to work.

When they weren't in school or church, they'd help me run the hoop nets and trotlines, or they'd help me haul fish up from the riverbank. During the summers, they'd help me churn out duck calls on the lathe, a hefty piece of hot-running equipment that was housed in a rusty metal shack. It was hard, sweaty, and low-paying labor, and times being what they were, we didn't have a lot of discretionary money lying around. I was able to give them all they needed, of course, but if they wanted something, they had to work hard and save their money. Industry and frugality, I taught them, went hand in hand.

Day after day they joined me in my labor, and conscious of the little eyes and ears around me, I refrained from cursing or using the name of the Almighty in vain. As we went, I taught them the gospel, how Christ had come to earth, died for our sins, and conquered death. I taught them that a commitment to the life of Christ meant a commitment to keep his words, to pattern our lives after his. We were to be moral, generous, hospitable folks. We were to be Christian.

I taught them to work hard and save their money. I taught them to live moral lives. But I taught them to be kind and respectful to others too. I forbade them from sassing Miss Kay and they wouldn't have considered sassing me. They were also taught to respect their teachers at school and church. They were warned against lashing out in anger and told that if they came to blows, there'd be swift punishment by the man of the house—me.

It wasn't all work and no play, though. I taught them that the Almighty had given us his nature to steward and enjoy. And what could be more enjoyable than duck hunting? Each winter we'd make our way to the blinds, and we'd share a few laughs before harvesting a few birds. We enjoyed each other, and after every hunt I'd remind the boys of my idea of the good life: profitable work, a good wife, a strong family, and a little duck hunting.

Could you ask for anything more?

I taught my boys to follow the Scriptures, keep their lives

straight, love their fellow man, do what's right, work hard on the river, and hunt ducks. The way I saw it, if they did this, their lives would be happy, happy, happy. They'd live good lives, have stable families, and find peace of mind just like I had. If they didn't follow these principles, though, if they decided to leave the virtuous life, especially while living under my roof, they'd come up empty. They'd never find peace. How'd I know? Simple. I'd be the one to disrupt their tranquility. And could there be a more effective way of disrupting a son's tranquility than through his hindquarters?

The Robertson penal code was simple. Run afoul of biblical living? Three licks. (A form of punishment, by the way, that's fallen out of favor with the left-wingers these days.) No more. No less. Only three.

Dishonor your mother? Three licks.

Disrespect your teacher? Three licks.

Get caught drinking, cursing, or punching your brother. Three licks, three licks, three licks.

Each time, I reminded them that Robertsons were committed to the Almighty, and the Almighty wanted us to be virtuous, upright people. I also reminded them that there was no way to live a life of perfect virtue, try as we might, and that those three licks were just a reminder that every sin has its penalty, even if we ultimately walk into God's forgiveness.

All in all, the boys were straight arrows, especially when they were young, but I knew that at some point, at least one of them would try to get away with some stuff. But here's something all good duckmen know: you can't slick the old dog, the one that knows all the tricks. I was the old dog. Al was the first one who tried to slick me.

Al was the oldest, and he'd experienced the worst of my wild days. He hadn't had a proper father figure for a good chunk of his childhood, and I suppose he resented me a little for my early absence in his life. As he grew older, he tested me by wading into the waters of defiance. For a season he chased freedom, just like I had, and in the beginning of those years, when he was just in high school, he started running with a few hellions, unruly boys who drank and cussed and generally raised a ruckus everywhere they went.

One afternoon Miss Kay came down to the shop and told me I had a phone call. It was one of the mamas of Al's running buddies. She'd discovered that Al, her son, and a couple of others were down at duck camp drinking beer. She hadn't authorized her boy to drink beer, she said, and she knew I hadn't given Al permission either. Without a husband around, though, she didn't have anyone who could knock some sense into her son. She needed a little help.

I told her I'd go down to camp and put an end to the beer drinking, but before I did, I asked whether she'd let me give him a dose of discipline. She agreed, then gave me the phone numbers for the other mothers. I called each of them, told them I'd be heading down to discipline Al and one of his buddies, then offered my fatherly services to them too. They all agreed. I was about to bring the thunder.

I rolled down to the camp just after noon and stood in the front yard outside the tiny shack. I guess the boys heard my truck rumbling down the dirt road, because before I said a word I could see them peeking through the window blinds. I hollered at them and told them I'd gotten a bad report downriver and I knew they'd been drinking beer. I told Al he'd best be out for his licks within three minutes, and if the rest of them ever wanted to see Al again, they'd need to come get their licks too.

It didn't take three minutes.

Al came out first, hungover and dragging like a whipped pup. Raised as he was, he knew the drill. Disobedience to the Robertson family virtues (which were biblical virtues) brought swift, sure, but always fair punishment.

"You know what you did, son?" I asked.

"Yessir," he said.

"Take what's coming."

Al bent over the tailgate, and he took his three licks like a man before slinking to the side of the truck. I turned, looked at the other boys, and told them the Robertson clan tried their best to live by the Book, and the Book says to avoid drunkenness. If they wanted to keep running with Al or any of the other Robertson boys, they'd need to take their licks just like Al had. They looked at me sideways, all of them hesitating, all of them wondering whether I was bluffing.

"I ain't bluffing," I said. "Your mamas sent and authorized me."

If there's one thing a Southern boy is raised to do, it's respect his mama, and each of those boys knew what he had to do. One by one, they took their turns in the lick'n line. I told them I'd better not get another report of them carrying on and drinking, told them they'd need to straighten up and fly right.

Guess what? My licks left an indelible mark, though it wasn't the kind the left-wingers might think. Years passed and one by one those boys came back around to the Robertson house. One by one, they told me their lives had spun out of control, that they needed some order and stability, order like I had in my own life. One by one, I took them down to the river and baptized them. And almost twenty years after that event, the last of them came to the house, and after he came up out of the water, he thanked me for taking a stand for biblical virtues all those years ago. When he decided to live right, he said, he knew exactly where to go to find the answers for life—to the family who'd stood for godliness many years ago.

In an attempt to become more "civilized," society has told us that spanking is cruel. They've said spanking is bad for a child's psyche, that it'll ruin their self-esteem. They've called it uncivilized. They've said it's abuse, and sure, there are some who exceed the Robertson three-lick penalty, some who unfairly use the rod. But in dismissing God's wisdom about using the rod on disobedient children, in trying to adopt kinder, gentler forms of punishment without God, the children of today have run amok. Without God, see, all the civilization in the world won't produce an ounce of fruit.

In America we pretend to be the most civilized people on the planet. We wear fine suits, eat the best foods. We have all the extras life could offer—*lagniappe* as we call it down here in Louisiana. But what is civilization without virtue? A nightmare. Need proof? Look around.

See all the outrage, anger, and hatred. Doesn't it feel like it's getting worse, like society is spinning out of control?

Politicians are increasingly uncivil, disrespectful, and generally lacking in virtue. They attack their opponents with shameless name-calling, the occasional far-fetched allegation, and even lie to get their way. (For the record, though it's true I endorsed President Trump in the last election cycle, he's been guilty of just this kind of distasteful behavior. See? I'm nothing if not fair and balanced.) What does this kind of conduct say to our children and grandchildren?

This same incivility spills out into our streets too. Protest after protest makes the news, and I watch as men and women of all colors and creeds take to the streets. During the writing of this book, a group of neo-Nazis took to the streets of Charlottesville for the express purpose of raising a racist ruckus. Their sin opened the door to a group of counterprotesters, folks from the surrounding area who wanted the neo-Nazis run out of town on a rail (as all neo-Nazis should be). Some of those counterprotestors also turned to violence and incivility. The result? A young woman—a peaceful protestor by all accounts—was mowed down in the streets by one of those neo-Nazi types in an act of pure evil. This is the result of incivility: death.

I've never turned on a computer, and I only know how to pronounce the word *internet* because my children and grandchildren have told me all about it. I haven't the foggiest clue about social media, but I've been told that it's a cesspool of anger, outrage, disrespect, and incivility. It's also a covetous place, I'm told, a place where everyone shows off their stuff or envies other people's stuff.

The internet is also a place of rampant pornography, promiscuity, and sexual immorality. So much of it is anything but virtuous, I've been told, and more and more Americans seem to spend their time there.

If we only noticed a lack of virtue in our politics, protests, and on the internet, that'd be enough. But hasn't virtue all but left American culture? Haven't so many in America become lazy, slothful, overweight people addicted to entertainment? Hasn't our society been plagued by addiction, by drunkenness and pill popping? Aren't we a nation of overconsumers, people in debt up to our eyeballs? Haven't we lost sight of justice and the rule of law? In short, haven't we lost sight of virtue? And haven't a bunch of folks who'd identify as Christians been guilty of this same loss of virtue?

God was declared dead, and in came the enemy with a new lie—*virtue died with the God you killed.* The great thief, murderer, and destroyer convinced us that the virtues of old—virtues like temperance, order, industry and hard work, peace, humility, and the like—are outdated. And with no objective truth to guide our behavior, with no God to govern our passions, we took the bait. Hook, line, and sinker.

Our Founding Fathers knew the value of virtue. Consider Ben Franklin, who tried his best to live by thirteen virtues, including the following six:

1. Silence— "Speak not but what may benefit others or yourself; avoid trifling conversation"
2. Frugality— "Make no expense but to do good to others or yourself; waste nothing"

3. Industry— "Lose no time; be always employ'd in something useful; cut off all unnecessary actions"
4. Justice— "Wrong none by doing injuries, or omitting the benefits that are your duty"
5. Tranquility— "Be not disturbed at trifles, or at accidents common or unavoidable"
6. Humility— "Imitate Jesus and Socrates"[1]

What's more, he knew the source and supremacy of those virtues and morals, stating, "As to Jesus of Nazareth, my opinion of whom you particularly desire, I think the system of morals and His religion as He left them to us, the best the world ever saw or is likely to see."[2]

Likewise, our first president, George Washington, knew virtue and morality couldn't exist without the influence of God. In his farewell address of 1796, Washington said, "Whatever may be conceded to the influence of refined education on minds of peculiar structure, reason and experience both forbid us to expect that national morality can prevail in exclusion of religious principle." What religious principle did he mean? Of virtue and character he wrote, "To the distinguished character of Patriot, it should be our highest glory to add the more distinguished character of Christian."[3]

John Adams—Founding Father, first vice president, and second president—chimed in too, knowing that without God our society would spin into virtueless chaos. He wrote, "Without religion, this world would be something not fit to be mentioned in polite company: I mean hell." And if a world without religion would be hell, what would be its opposite? In his diary entry dated February 22, 1756, Adams wrote:

> Suppose a nation in some distant region should take the Bible for their only law book, and every member should regulate his conduct by the precepts there exhibited. Every member would be obliged in conscience to temperance and frugality and industry, to justice and kindness and charity towards his fellow men, and to piety and love and reverence toward almighty God. . . . What a Eutopia, what a Paradise would this region be.[4]

In other words, Adams believed that if our country relied on the Scriptures, if we allowed the Bible to regulate our government and its citizens, we would live in a more virtuous civilization. We'd be sober, frugal, hardworking, law-abiding, kind, generous, reverent, and loving people. Doesn't that sound like the kind of country you'd want to live in? It sounds like the closest thing to heaven we could experience this side of death if you ask me.

The Founding Fathers knew that a virtueless society could not prosper. They knew that without virtues we'd slide into corruption, laziness, incivility, and ultimately chaos. They also knew the Bible had quite a bit to say about virtue. Their divinely inspired wisdom was spot on.

There's never been a more perfect book of virtues than the Bible. Why? Because it provides more than just a blueprint for the virtuous life. It shows us how to perfectly embody godly virtues through the person of Christ. What's more, that same Christ—God with us—promised we could live a life of godly virtues through the help of the Holy Spirit.

That all sounds great, you say, but what does the Bible have to say about virtue?

I'm glad you asked. Let's look at a few examples, and for kicks, let's break them out according to John Adams's list.

TEMPERANCE (SELF-CONTROL)

We live in a world of runaway desire, of folks chasing their every addiction. The Bible, though, teaches the virtue of temperance, or self-control.

In the Proverbs Solomon cautioned against overindulgence, writing, "If you find honey, eat just enough—too much of it, and you will vomit" (25:16). He continued, characterizing the man who lacks self-control as "a city whose walls are broken through" (v. 28). Seems about like today's America, doesn't it?

In the New Testament Paul urged us not to indulge every desire, but to "offer your bodies as a living sacrifice, holy and pleasing to God—this is your true and proper worship" (Rom. 12:1). To that end he wrote that we should put on Christ, clothe ourselves in his self-control, and "not think about how to gratify the desires of the flesh" (13:14). Likewise, Peter wrote that followers of Christ should be sober-minded so that we might avoid the Devil who "prowls around like a roaring lion looking for someone to devour" (1 Peter 5:8).

What about the unvirtuous who lack self-control? Paul warned, "Do not be deceived: neither the immoral, nor idolaters, nor adulterers, nor sexual perverts, nor thieves, nor the greedy, nor drunkards, nor revilers, nor robbers will inherit the kingdom of God" (1 Cor. 6:9–10 RSV). See? The inability to practice self-control in every area—sexuality, the use of money, the use of wine—leads to death, destruction, and ultimate torment.

FRUGALITY

Merriam-Webster—the dictionary first compiled by Noah Webster, a godly man and the father of American education—defines *frugality* as being "characterized by or reflecting economy in the use of resources." Think the Bible has something to say about how to use our resources?

In the Proverbs Solomon cautioned against spending all our money on our own desires. He wrote, "Whoever loves pleasure will become poor; whoever loves wine and olive oil will never be rich" (21:17). In contrast, "the wise store up choice food and olive oil, but fools gulp theirs down" (v. 20). The wise make wise financial decisions and steward their resources well. They spend for their needs, maybe a want or two, and save the rest for a rainy day. And if the rain never comes, their economic wisdom becomes an inheritance for their children (13:22).

Jesus also preached against waste, greed, and selfish spending. In the gospel of Luke, he said, "Watch out! Be on your guard against all kinds of greed; life does not consist in an abundance of possessions" (12:15). Likewise, in his great Sermon on the Mount, he said, "Do not store up for yourselves treasures on earth, where moths and vermin destroy, and where thieves break in and steal. But store up for yourselves treasures in heaven, where moths and vermin do not destroy, and where thieves do not break in and steal" (Matt. 6:19–20). See? Jesus taught that the most economical use of our resources was to serve the kingdom of God, the kingdom that lasts forever.

INDUSTRY (HARD WORK)

The Bible has no shortage of teaching on industry and hard work. In his book of wisdom, Solomon addressed the virtue of hard work: "Those who work their land will have abundant food, but those who chase fantasies have no sense," and "Diligent hands will rule, but laziness ends in forced labor" (Prov. 12:11, 24). In Proverbs 13:4 he likewise wrote, "A sluggard's appetite is never filled, but the desires of the diligent are fully satisfied." In Proverbs 14:23 he wrote, "All hard work brings a profit, but mere talk leads only to poverty."

Paul echoed these instructions to the Ephesians: Thieves "must steal no longer, but must work, doing something useful with their own hands, that they may have something to share with those in need" (4:28). To the Colossians Paul issued a similar instruction: "Whatever you do, work at it with all your heart, as working for the Lord, not for human masters" (3:23).

JUSTICE

Anyone with a C knowledge of the Bible knows that the Almighty loves justice. Throughout the Old Testament he reminds his people of the importance of creating a just, ordered, and law-abiding society.

In the book of Proverbs, Solomon showed how a just society flourishes. He wrote, "When justice is done, it brings joy to the righteous but terror to evildoers" (21:15). Likewise, he wrote, "Whoever says to the guilty, 'You are innocent,' will be cursed by peoples and denounced by nations. But it will go well with those who convict the guilty, and rich blessing will come on them" (24:24–25).

The Psalms likewise contain promises for those who follow justice. In Psalm 37:27–28 the psalmist wrote, "Turn from evil and do good; then you will dwell in the land forever. For the LORD loves the just and will not forsake his faithful ones. Wrongdoers will be completely destroyed; the offspring of the wicked will perish." In Psalm 106:3 it's written, "Blessed are those who act justly, who always do what is right."

What happens when a people follow justice, when they pursue it at all costs? Isaiah recorded God's words: "Listen to me, my people; hear me, my nation: Instruction will go out from me; my justice will become a light to the nations" (Isa. 51:4). True justice, the justice of God, is a light that guides the paths of those who follow it. It leads them into peace, prosperity, and the favor of God.

KINDNESS

Christ came preaching the truth, and as hard as the truth could be, he preached it with the utmost kindness. He preached it to the religious leaders of the day, those who sought to kill him from the beginning. And these were not just political foes either; they were eternal, mortal enemies. Yet Christ did not stoop to slander. In fact, he preached against it on the Sermon on the Mount, saying, "Anyone who says to a brother or sister, 'Raca,' is answerable to the court. And anyone who says, 'You fool!' will be in danger of the fire of hell" (Matt. 5:22).

Likewise, Paul instructed the Ephesians to practice civility in their speech, even in the face of fierce opposition. Recognizing that opposition so often leads to anger and anger opens the door to temptation, he wrote, "In your anger do not sin . . . and do not give the devil a foothold" (4:26–27). Paul knew that anger often gives way to insults, to accusation, maybe even to slander. Knowing this, he followed this admonition with this counsel: "Do not let any unwholesome talk come out of your mouths, but only what is helpful for building others up according to their needs, that it may benefit those who listen" (v. 29). To take it a step further, he wrote, "Be kind and compassionate to one another, forgiving each other, just as in Christ God forgave you" (v. 32).

See? Paul knew unwholesome insults spoken in anger—uncivil speech—wouldn't benefit the listener. It wouldn't change anyone's mind. What will change hearts and minds though? Kindness. And for the record, that's a godly virtue. As the Scriptures say, it's God's kindness that leads to our own repentance (Rom. 2:4).

CHARITY (LOVING ONE ANOTHER)

These days it seems like so many are out for themselves. They've forgotten how to sacrifice their own desires for the good of their fellow man. This is what the virtue of biblical charity is all about—sacrificial love. Did anyone do this better than Christ, the man who gave his life to pay for our sins? Consider his most charitable command: "A new command I give you: Love one another. As I have loved you, so you must love one another" (John 13:34). Do you think a love like Jesus', one that gives of itself for the sake of the world, would make a difference in America? I do.

The Scriptures have plenty to say about the virtuous life. They speak to being sober, wise managers of money, hardworking, just, kind, and loving, both to men and God. The Devil would have us believe the lie that these virtues are outdated, and the result is nothing short of chaos. As proof, you only need to look to those politicians under his control. Don't they love their uncivil speech, mocking and insulting each other at every turn? Don't they mismanage money, running up our deficit year after year? Aren't so many of them caught in sexual scandals, unable to be self-controlled and sober? And what about the people of this country? Don't we resemble our politicians?

Consider it: If we lived a life of virtue as described in the Bible, wouldn't it change the course of our country? Wouldn't our opioid epidemic, our drunkenness, and the effects of our sexual immorality be a distant memory if we practiced self-control? Wouldn't our hard work and frugality save us from the burdens of a welfare state and maybe lead to a reduction of our national debt? Wouldn't we be kinder to one another, only saying things that would help each other? Wouldn't the chaotic violence spilling into the streets stop if we were committed to justice, civility, and loving one another? In short, wouldn't it be John Adams's utopia?

You bet.

American Christian: you have the responsibility to be a model of virtue. Be salt and light. Only through godly virtue can the people of God bring heaven to earth. Who doesn't want that?

While filming *Duck Dynasty,* I had the privilege of meeting some of those New York City muckety-mucks in the entertainment industry. From time to time they'd come down to West Monroe to spend time with Miss Kay and me. They wanted to get to know us, to see whether we were the real deal. And when they came, we'd put on a big pot of duck gumbo or jambalaya or crawfish étouffée. We'd stuff them with pralines or Miss Kay's fried pies, and we'd sit around the table and talk. Of course I took every opportunity to share the good news of Jesus with them, but we didn't just talk about Jesus. We'd talk business or politics or entertainment—whatever might come up in the course of conversation.

Sitting across the table from one of those executives, I asked whether I could hazard a guess as to how *Duck Dynasty* had found its way to their network. The way I figured it, I said, a group of executives like him were sitting around a table, and one of them proposed filming a reality show about a functional, hardworking family that'd made a name for themselves. I reckoned they needed a family of character and full of characters, one without a hint of scandal. I took it a step further and guessed that someone in that room had asked, "Where in the world will we find a family like that?"

I paused and asked if I had it about right.

He was smiling, nodding along.

"And then you found a bunch of decent river rats making duck calls down here in Northern Louisiana, and you were all intrigued. Am I close?"

"That's about it," he said.

"How's that worked out for you?" I asked.

He just smiled. That smile, the merchandizing proceeds, and the *Duck Dynasty* ratings answered the question.

During the *Duck Dynasty* years, I'm sure there were some viewers who found the Robertson family odd. They probably tuned in for the novelty of a bunch of Bible-thumping, shotgun tote'n, beard-wear'n, duck call make'n dudes who'd married virtuous women way above their pay grades. I reckon some of those viewers found our practice of biblical virtues peculiar. But as they watched, here's what they witnessed: a family committed to living a life of biblical virtue. They saw how that kind of family enjoys stability, peace of mind, family order, and prosperity. In short, they saw the fruit of living by the Almighty's commands. And if the ratings were any indication, they were hungry for it.

The American people are mired in an unprecedented time of instability, incivility, and regular chaos. Their families are broken. Kindness is in short supply. Without self-control they're addicted, and the orgasm is the pinnacle of their daily experience. They'll lie, cheat, and steal, or be hurt by those who lie, cheat, or steal. Why? Simple. America has fallen for the enemy's lie, the lie that biblical virtues are outdated.

Without virtue America has no moral authority, and without moral authority can we survive? I don't think so. But where will we turn to learn virtues?

The entertainment industry in Hollywood, California? No way.

The news desks in New York City? Nope.

The politicians and policy makers in Washington, DC? Nah.

There's only one source of true virtue, a source that's been time-tested—the Bible. Its code is simple and true: don't be a drunkard or drug addict; spend your money wisely; work hard; promote justice and law and order; be kind to others, always civil; love your neighbor. Friend, if you'd save yourself, turn from the lie of the evil one, trust Jesus, and commit yourself to the truth of biblical virtue. If you do, you'll inspire others to follow suit, and if enough people follow along, maybe we'll find our way to John Adams's utopia. Maybe we'll find our way to heaven on earth.

THE LIE: LAWS CAN BE IGNORED OR
CHANGED IF THEY ARE INCONVENIENT.

THE TRUTH: LAW AND ORDER COME
FROM THE WORD OF GOD.

My morning routine is regular. Unwavering. Predictable.

After I wake up and throw on my daily camo, I make my way to the coffeepot and fill it with filtered water so as not to pollute my coffee flavor with chlorine. *Merriam-Webster* defines *chlorine* as "a greenish yellow, poisonous, gaseous chemical element having a disagreeable odor." I don't take my coffee with cream or sugar, and I'd rather not take it with poisonous gas either.

After I pour the water in, I load it up with grounds. "How much?" you ask. As many as it'll hold, dude. I like my coffee strong, blacker than midnight. I don't want to see the bottom of my cup, and I don't want it covered over in whipped cream either. If you ask me, one of the primary lies that threatens to steal the soul of America is this: European-named, lightly tinted brown water filled with sugar and topped with a whipped cream swirl is the same thing as coffee.

There should be a law against such things.

After a few cups of sturdy coffee, I leave the house, and when I get to the end of my driveway, I'm faced with a decision. Should I take a left and make my way to town on the wider road, or should I take a right and head down the narrower road that eventually leads to the woods. The road I don't often take, the road to town, is wider and better paved. It leads us to places like the grocery store, or church, or Miss Kay's Eats & Sweets—all fine and good places. But those roads also lead to the population centers, the places of hustle and bustle and European-named coffee. They lead away from the quieter fields of God and into the metropolises of men, places where folks often chase their own desires. Maybe that's why I avoid it. Many of those roads lead to the virtueless places of American society. So, as you might guess, nine times out of ten, I take the narrow road to the woods.

There are two seasons in Louisiana: duck season and off-season. In duck season the narrow roads lead me to my flooded fields and the blinds, and there I set out the decoys and prepare for a harvest. In the off-season, though, the season when the fields aren't flooded, I ride around the fields in my Yamaha and tend to my plot. I take out undesirable weeds that choke out the good grasses and cut down the trees that will eventually block my shooting lanes. I survey the water levels or take out the beaver dams that'll keep the fields from flooding at the right time. As I work in the quietness of the great outdoors, there's a fragrant peace.

As narrow as the road is that leads me into the woods—only wide enough for my Yamaha—there are narrow paths, pig trails that feral hogs and wild game use to get from field to stream. These narrow trails lead to feeding grounds or places where the deer bed down. They lead to watering holes or the beavers' den. These are some of my favorite places in the woods because they support so much innocent life. I can spend hours just watching these trails, and as I do, guess what? I live a sin-free life.

Alone in the woods, it's possible to go a whole day without sinning, nutty as that may sound. Walking alone in the fields and praying, watching the game running up and down the pig trails, it's unlikely you'll use the Lord's name in vain or worship some other god. In the woods there's no one to steal from, no women to lust after. There's no one to lie to either, and you can't murder someone who's not around. Sin management in isolation is easy, see.

I suspect our Founding Fathers knew most people wouldn't participate in sin management by making their way to the woods. They knew that our great America wouldn't be forged in isolation, and that most people would congregate down the wider roads. They knew folks would rub shoulders as they built the great society. And as I wrote in the previous chapter, they hoped these folks—together with all their children and grandchildren—would build a strong and virtuous nation. They knew, though, that any community of people hoping to build a virtuous society would need a teacher. And so they left us the ultimate instructor: a canon of biblically based law.

God created us to live in relationship with him and each other. He created us in love for love. But even from the beginning, men had trouble living with one another, much less loving one another. Eve tricked Adam. Cain killed Abel. A whole world of folks in Noah's day and age were violent and unruly. Without some code, some law or governing authority of men, they were bent on evil.

After the Almighty freed his people from Egypt, he knew

they'd need some code, some set of laws if they were going to make it. So, in his graciousness, the one Lawgiver and Judge himself gave his people an exact, objective standard to govern their conduct. He gave them a tool to instruct them on how to build a godly and loving society. What was that tool? The law.

In the Exodus account, we find God's people wandering in the desert. Freed from the tyrannical rule of Egypt's pharaoh, they were forming a new nation. Knowing this nation would need a code of conduct, rules for leading them into understanding their relationship to God and one another, God called Moses to Mount Sinai, and he gave them ten simple laws written on stone tablets. What were those ten laws?

1. You shall have no other gods before me.
2. You shall not make for yourself an image in the form of anything in heaven above or on the earth beneath or in the waters below. You shall not bow down to them or worship them.
3. You shall not misuse the name of the LORD your God, for the LORD will not hold anyone guiltless who misuses his name.
4. Remember the Sabbath day by keeping it holy. Six days you shall labor and do all your work, but the seventh day is a Sabbath to the LORD your God.
5. Honor your father and your mother, so that you may live long in the land the LORD your God is giving you.
6. You shall not murder.
7. You shall not commit adultery.

8. You shall not steal.

9. You shall not give false testimony against your neighbor.

10. You shall not covet your neighbor's house. You shall not covet your neighbor's wife, or his male or female servant, his ox or donkey, or anything that belongs to your neighbor.

The law was given to the people of Israel to teach them how to love both God and their neighbors. It was the basis of their well-ordered society. Truth is, those Ten Commandments probably didn't contain any real surprises—honor God alone; don't kill; don't steal; don't lie; respect your parents; don't cheat on your wife. Common sense should tell you these things will help a society run more smoothly. Still, God gave them the written law as a reminder for when the people of Israel were tempted to stray. The law served as their guide, or as Paul wrote in his letter to the Galatians, it was their "guardian until Christ came" (3:24).

Simple as it was, did the Israelites follow God's law?

Nah.

Time and time again, God's people ignored the law and chased their own desires. They lied, cheated, and stole from the poor. They chased sex, coveted their neighbors' wives. Time after time, they worshiped idols. They forgot the ways of God or otherwise justified their sins, and so, time and time again, God sent prophets to remind the nation of Israel of the consequences of breaking the law. In fact, one of the last instructions given in the entire Old Testament came from one of those prophets, Malachi, who recorded God's words,

"Remember the law of my servant Moses, the decrees and laws I gave him" (Mal. 4:4).

It wasn't just the prophets who reminded the Israelites of the law and its purpose though. King Solomon wrote of the law's purpose in the book of Proverbs. He reminded his readers there were things God truly hated, writing,

> There are six things the LORD hates,
>> seven that are detestable to him:
>>> haughty eyes,
>>> a lying tongue,
>>> hands that shed innocent blood,
>>> a heart that devises wicked schemes,
>>> feet that are quick to rush into evil,
>>> a false witness who pours out lies
>>> and a person who stirs up conflict in the community.
>>>> (6:16–19)

How could the people avoid the things the Almighty hated—the lying, murder, and wickedness? Simple. They could listen to the law of Moses as passed down from their mothers and fathers. Solomon wrote,

> My son, keep your father's command
>> and do not forsake your mother's teaching.
> Bind them always on your heart;
>> fasten them around your neck.
>>> (vv. 20–21)

And Solomon promised that if the people avoided the things the Almighty hated and obeyed his instructions, the law would watch over them when they slept, speak to them when they awoke, guide them like a lamp, and show them the way to life (vv. 22–23). When followed, the law would bring peace with God and their neighbors.

But what about those who weren't Israelites? What about the Gentiles, whether Roman, Greek, or otherwise? How could they order their lives? After all, they didn't have the law. Right? It is true that the Gentiles were not under the law of Moses, but Paul recognized there are certain absolute truths all people know. There is something in all people that shows them right from wrong. He wrote,

> Indeed, when Gentiles, who do not have the law, do by nature things required by the law, they are a law for themselves, even though they do not have the law. They show that the requirements of the law are written on their hearts, their consciences also bearing witness, and their thoughts sometimes accusing them and at other times even defending them. (Rom. 2:14–15)

And just as the law of the Israelites was meant to guide the people in learning to love God and each other, the law written on people's hearts could be summed up in one word: *love*. Paul wrote,

> Let no debt remain outstanding, except the continuing debt to love one another, for whoever loves others has fulfilled the law. The commandments, "You shall not commit adultery," "You shall

not murder," "You shall not steal," "You shall not covet," and whatever other command there may be, are summed up in this one command: "Love your neighbor as yourself." Love does no harm to a neighbor. Therefore love is the fulfillment of the law. (Rom. 13:8–10)

In other words, if people simply acted in love toward others, they wouldn't violate any of the Ten Commandments. They wouldn't lie, cheat, or steal.

See how powerful love is?

Our Founding Fathers understood the value of the law of Moses. They knew that any group of people living together would have difficulty living the perfect law of love, so they framed our republic with the timbers of biblical truth, biblical law. They knew that only by living godly lives—lives ordered by God's laws—would we ever achieve lasting peace and prosperity.

I can already hear the left-wingers getting all upset. I can see them wringing their hands. I already know what they'll say: *Our Founding Fathers never intended to build a governing framework, a framework of laws on biblical truth.*

Agree to disagree, dude.

How do I know the Founding Fathers based our canon of law on the Bible? Consider their words.

John Adams wrote,

The general principles, on which the Fathers achieved independence, were the only Principles in which that beautiful Assembly of young Gentlemen could Unite. . . . And what were these general Principles? I answer, the general Principles of Christianity, in which all these Sects were United: And the general Principles of English and American Liberty, in which all those young Men United, and which had United all Parties in America, in Majorities sufficient to assert and maintain her Independence. Now I will avow, that I then believe, and now believe, that those general Principles of Christianity, are as eternal and immutable, as the Existence and Attributes of God; and that those Principles of Liberty, are as unalterable as human Nature and our terrestrial, mundane System.[1]

And as I wrote in the previous chapter, Adams also believed a system of laws based on God's Word would lead to a virtuous "Utopia."

Patrick Henry wrote, "The great pillars of all government and of social life . . . [are] virtue, morality, and religion. This is the armor, my friend, and this alone, that renders us invincible."[2] What religion was he referencing? Henry was a devout Christian, a follower of the Scriptures who left a last will and testament that said, "This is all the inheritance I give to my dear family. The religion of Christ will give them one which will make them rich indeed."[3]

Likewise, signer of the Constitution James McHenry believed that only a biblically based legal system could secure the peace of America. He wrote,

Public utility pleads . . . for the general distribution of the Holy Scriptures. The doctrine they preach—the obligations they impose—the punishment they threaten—the rewards they promise—the stamp and image of divinity they bear which produces a conviction of their truths—[these] can alone secure to society, order and peace, and to our courts of justice and constitutions of government, purity, stability, and usefulness. In vain, without the Bible, we increase penal laws and draw entrenchments around our institutions. Bibles are strong entrenchments. Where they abound, men cannot pursue wicked courses.[4]

John Quincy Adams, the sixth president of the United States, indicated "[t]he Declaration of Independence first organized the social compact on the foundation of the Redeemer's mission upon earth . . . [and] laid the cornerstone of human government upon the first precepts of Christianity."[5] He also stated, "The law given from Sinai was a civil and municipal as well as a moral and religious code . . . laws essential to the existence of men in society, and most of which have been enacted by every nation, which ever professed any code of laws."[6]

Signer of the Constitution William Patterson said, "Religion and morality . . . [are] necessary to good government, good order, and good laws."[7] Noah Webster wrote, "Where will you find any code of laws among civilized men in which the commands and prohibitions are not founded on Christian principles?"[8] The evidence is overwhelming. These men intended American society to be built on a Christian set of laws.

It wasn't just the Founding Fathers who claimed the legal system of the United States was based on the biblical law. The belief that American law was based on Judeo-Christian principles has been passed down through the ages. Consider, too, the statement by one of our earliest Supreme Court justices, Joseph Story, who in a speech at Harvard University in 1829 said,

> I verily believe Christianity necessary to the support of civil society. One of the beautiful boasts of our municipal jurisprudence is that Christianity is a part of the Common Law. . . . There never has been a period in which the Common Law did not recognize Christianity as laying its foundations. I verily believe Christianity necessary to the support of civil society.[9]

In 1883 the Illinois Supreme Court stated,

> Our laws and our institutions must necessarily be based upon and embody the teachings of the Redeemer of mankind. It is impossible that it should be otherwise; and in this sense and to this extent our civilization and our institutions are emphatically Christian. . . . This is a Christian nation.[10]

On February 15, 1950, President Harry S. Truman addressed the Attorney General's Conference on Law Enforcement Problems, stating, "The fundamental basis of this Nation's law was given to Moses on the Mount. The fundamental basis of our Bill of Rights comes from the teachings which we get from Exodus and St. Matthew, from Isaiah and St. Paul."[11] And in a proclamation dated February 3, 1983, President Ronald Reagan declared,

Of the many influences that have shaped the United States of America into a distinctive Nation and people, none may be said to be more fundamental and enduring than the Bible. . . . The Bible and its teachings helped form the basis for the Founding Fathers' abiding belief in the inalienable rights of the individual, rights which they found implicit in the Bible's teachings of the inherent worth and dignity of each individual. This same sense of man patterned the convictions of those who framed the English system of law inherited by our own Nation, as well as the ideals set forth in the Declaration of Independence and the Constitution.[12]

Over and over, the leaders of our country have recognized the importance of the Bible in framing our legal system. They knew it was the perfect source of law. They've indicated it is what makes us a distinctive people. Ultimately, they knew that any society that lives up to that standard is a society that has a shot. But although they never said it, I suspect most of those Founding Fathers didn't see the Bible as a simple book of philosophy or of rules for ordering society. I imagine they knew there was an ultimate aim of the law—to teach us how to live together in godly love and peace.

It seems straightforward, if you ask me. And yet, having convinced us that God is dead, that there is no absolute truth, and that virtue is outdated, the evil one has managed to undermine the very basis of our law. If there is no perfect Lawgiver, then there can be no perfect law. If there is no absolute truth, then how can there be any absolute law? If virtue is outdated, how can our system of laws ensure a virtuous society? The enemy has attacked our very legal system with his insidious lies, and he's topped those lies with yet another: *laws that are inconvenient, that get in the way of our personal pleasure, can be changed.* After all, why can't we change laws that aren't based on something timeless and true?

The result? Death. Destruction. Degradation in our quality of living.

In chapter 4 I wrote about these consequences as it relates to abortion, how after we declared God dead and began to question his absolute truth, we declared that a woman had a constitutional right to terminate human life. Now, we terminate unborn babies with regularity. And just as we've moved the legal lines to encourage sinful behavior like abortion, we've used the law as a barrier to keep God out too. The courts have declared it is unconstitutional for teachers and principals to lead Christian prayer in public school, despite the fact that our Founding Fathers often prayed together while they were founding this country. What's the result? We've certainly seen a rise in violence, drug use, and mass shootings in public schools since the 1960s and '70s.

See? Death. Destruction. Degradation in our quality of living.

And what's the ultimate sign that we've bought the Devil's lie hook, line, and sinker? The Supreme Court has declared that judges and courthouses cannot publicly display the Ten Commandments, an especially odd decision since a likeness of Moses carrying the Ten Commandments is displayed on the frieze in the Supreme Court building. Odd, too, because the Ten Commandments are the very law that forms the foundation of our legal system, at least the best I can tell from reading the writings of historical leaders of our country. And consider this: Could there be any better place to display the Ten Commandments other than the very courthouse where a criminal will be tried and convicted for lying, stealing, or killing? I don't think so.

Then again, maybe that's just river-rat logic.

America has bought the lie that its legal system is not based on God's law and that it can be changed to accommodate its desires. As I look around, I'd say the result of those changes is both evident and tragic. They've paved the way for the theft of America's soul.

As long as men aren't living in isolation, the law is an important tool. It shows men the rules, helps them build a well-ordered, properly functioning society. It instructs them in how to live virtuous lives. God knew this. The Israelites knew this. The Founding Fathers knew this.

Now don't get me wrong; our Founding Fathers didn't always make perfectly biblical laws. They knew the Scriptures, and based on those Scriptures, they wrote that "all men are created equal, that they are endowed by their Creator with certain unalienable rights." Despite their recognition of this fundamental truth that all men were created equal—the truth embodied by the Scriptures in the statement that there is neither slave nor free in Christ—they participated in the sin of slavery. They took the lands of the natives under the doctrine of Manifest Destiny. Still, they understood that a truly just society would never emerge if it didn't have the Word of God as its starting place, because without the Bible there's no foundation for the absolute truth. There's no truth that calls people to repent from participating in corrupt laws.

Despite what our forefathers intended, modern Americans— including many in the church—have bought the lie that our country's laws aren't based on some sure and certain foundation. We've blurred the lines of the law or moved them. The Supreme Court of these United States has declared that same-sex marriage is legally permissible, and as I'm writing this book, they're mulling over whether a Christian baker has the right to refuse services to a same-sex couple getting married. The way I understand it—a C+ river rat's understanding—the baker refused to bake the cake because he believes same-sex marriage constitutes sinful behavior. Why does he think that? Because the Bible says it. Now, make no mistake about it, I don't hate any member of the gay community. In fact, I love them and want them to know the truth of God's Word, how it might set them free. So, though I would bake the cake for the couple, I wouldn't write anything on it that would make me compromise the truth of God's law—that marriage is between a man and woman. And if the couple asked why, I'd tell them it's because the law of God is unchanging. In the same way, I wouldn't approve of any message on a cake that celebrated lying, stealing, murder, children disobeying parents, depravity, greed, strife, deceit, malice, slander, insolent behavior, arrogance, boastfulness, or any other sexually immoral or perverted conduct. (That's the list pulled straight from Romans 1:29–30, in case you were wondering.) I can't approve of any of these behaviors, no matter what human laws say, because they're contrary to the biblical law.

You can't simply call something marriage that's not recognized as marriage by the Almighty. That's the kind of law changing that would make the Founding Fathers roll over in their graves. But it's not just the changing definition of marriage. We've blurred so many legal lines. Sure, murder may be illegal, but we've believed that we could change the legal definition of murder so it doesn't apply to the unborn. But a simple change in the legal definition of what constitutes murder (or what constitutes human life for that matter) does not make it so. In the same way, legalizing a union between two men or two women does not change God's legal definition of marriage. Legalizing dope doesn't make intoxication legal under the law of the Almighty. Changing the tax code or lobbying laws to give corporations more money, power, and control won't make greed, arrogance, or insolence legal according to God's law. You can't move the lines of divine law, at least not as far as God is concerned. And if you do? Get ready. We'll have a slaughterhouse, a den of thieves, a drug-infested, lusty Sodom and Gomorrah down here. Actually, maybe Sodom and Gomorrah aren't strong enough descriptions. Maybe I should say, it'll be a real modern-day America down here.

Instead of trying to rewrite our history or blur the lines of law, we need to look back to the faith of our forefathers and rededicate ourselves to living lives worthy of the legal system they set up. And yes, this starts in the church. This starts with Christian people remembering the absolute truth of God's Word, dedicating themselves to it, and living it out in love. This starts with the church reminding American society of our roots, our foundations. But it also begins with the church reminding those who've violated the law that Jesus offers forgiveness and freedom from guilt and shame. Through Jesus there's a way to return to the narrower paths of life. Because I believe this truth more than anything, I carry it with me everywhere I go. I share it with the lawless wherever I run up on them. Men in jail. Women on parole. Folks on the run from the law who come up on my property from time to time. I even share it with the law-changing heathens in Washington, DC (your senators and representatives). And on occasion, I've had the privilege of sharing the good news to a highly concentrated bunch of lawless men. (No, I'm not talking about an actors' convention in Hollywood, California.) On occasion, I've carried this good news of Jesus with me to Angola, the Louisiana State Penitentiary, also known as the Alcatraz of the South.

Angola, a prison just about twenty miles north of St. Francisville, is one of the hardest places in America. It serves as the home of murderers, rapists, and thieves. It has a dedicated death row. As of last count, more than five thousand inmates were behind its razor-wired walls.

I'd first been invited to Angola by warden Burl Cain, a man who knew how the power of Christ could change the lives of his inmates. He'd been an advocate for Christian-based programs in the prison and had allowed the inmates to construct a chapel on the prison grounds. When I arrived at the prison, Warden Cain invited me to the guesthouse, where they served an incredible meal, cooked and served by some of the better-behaved inmates, and it was capped off with lemon icebox pie that'd rival Miss Kay's. (Don't tell her I said so.) As we ate that pie, Warden Cain told me that many of the men in these walls would never see the outside. They'd come here to die. But still he believed the gospel of Jesus could give these lawbreakers great hope. In fact, he said he'd seen it firsthand. Men at Angola had accepted the gospel and been completely reformed. They stopped cursing the other inmates, stopped fighting and trying to break prison rules. Those who'd become gospel followers were model citizens in Angola. That's why he'd invited me, he said. More than a few of these men watched *Duck Dynasty*, and maybe they'd listen to the gospel message if it was preached by a celebrity. With that he led me to chapel where the inmates gathered.

There in front of the roughest crowd I'd ever seen, I told those men I knew why they were there. They were murderers, rapists, thieves. They were the ones who'd disobeyed God's laws, had broken the Ten Commandments that served as the basis of American law.

"Gentlemen, this is the end of the line for most of you," I said. "Most of you are going to die in this prison, but I have some good news for you. You can be under lock and key, but you can still be free."

I went on to share the good news to that group, told them if they renounced their law-breaking ways and followed Christ, they could be set free from the sin and shame of their heinous acts. What's more, they could have eternal life.

I closed my gospel presentation, and the men were dismissed. The warden brought in another group. Then another. I shared the good news of Jesus with every man who came through those chapel doors, and when I was finished, the warden brought me more good news. Some of those killers on death row, the ones who weren't permitted out of their cells, had heard my little sermon. The warden had streamed it through speakers into their cells. Some of those men, the vilest of all lawbreakers, heard the news: they could have a clean start as far as God was concerned.

In the days after I visited, I'd come to find out that more than a few men had accepted the good news. They'd come to a saving knowledge of Jesus and had been baptized in one of the irrigation lakes there at Angola. Their law-breaking records had been wiped clean in the eyes of the Almighty. They'd been set free, even if they couldn't avoid the consequences of their actions. Even if some of them might be executed for their crimes, when they awoke to the afterlife, they would be in a heavenly eternity.

Ironic as it is, all those Angola lawbreakers who accepted the good news of Jesus have found true freedom. So many outside of prisons, though, those who've disobeyed God's laws regarding marriage or abortion or smoking weed or cutting corners to make a little more money, are anything but free. Try as they might to blur the lines of the law, to change the laws that don't suit their pleasures, they can't avoid the punishment coming their way. If they asked— which they won't—I'd tell them that judgment is coming to them, just as surely as it's come to those in Angola. I'd tell them that the prisons like Angola are a veritable garden of Eden compared to the eternal prison that waits for them. I'd also tell them this: they can be set free from the judgment, just like those brothers in Angola.

American church, it's time to confront the lie that our system of law isn't based on God's law, that it can be changed to accommodate our desires. It's time to live that truth with integrity too. Don't participate in legalized murder, intoxication, fornication, or greed. Live according to godly law, and do your best to influence your legislators to do the same. Take this news to the prisons, the jailhouses, the juvenile corrections institutions: even when you break God's law, you can have forgiveness and freedom through Christ. Take the news to the streets too. Carry it down the wider roads that lead to the population centers of America. Tell the people that only a return to God's law will lead us into a more ordered and loving society, a life free of sin.

8

THE LIE: **UNITY IS NOT POSSIBLE.**

THE TRUTH: **UNITY FLOWS FROM
A GOD-CENTERED CULTURE.**

If you've heard me speak for more than ten minutes, you know this much about me: I've been clear about my view of politics. What's my view? Simple. No government program—whether health care, social security, or whatever—can save you. It may put food in your belly (at great expense). It may get you into the hospital (at even greater expense). It may provide for you in the dog days of your life. (How in the world can we afford all these programs?) No matter what it may or may not do, it will not save your soul. Only one thing will: Jesus. And so the way I figure, pouring our time, energy, and resources into the government is nothing more than spiritual waste.

My opinion, dude. Take it or leave it.

Outspoken as I've been about this truth over the years, I've been invited to speak at more than one political rally. And it's no secret that most of those rallies have been conservative in nature. It's no secret I've publicly endorsed candidates I thought might scale back government. It's also no secret I've spoken at rallies on behalf of candidates I've believed to be Christians. And sure, sometimes it backfires, but I take my responsibility to promote the people of God seriously. I also take my responsibility to share the good news seriously, so at every political rally I attend, I make sure to share the saving message of Jesus.

In the summer of 2017 I was asked to speak at a political event. I was told I could speak freely about government, guns, God, or whatever else might be on my mind. It'd be a sizable event, they said, and knowing I'd have a bunch of sitting ducks and could shotgun the good news of Jesus at them, I agreed. I hopped on a plane and made my way to the host's home state.

The event started like any other I'd attended. Folks in the crowd held up signs, chanted "USA," and cheered for the candidate, all things I expected. But then, a popular political operative took the stage on behalf of the candidate. That's when I noticed a shift. He knew which buttons to push, and he offered political solution after political solution. He didn't mention God's name a single time, but instead called out political opponents by name, conservative and liberal alike. He said we needed to clean house, needed to get rid of the establishment politicians in Washington, DC, who saw the people in that crowd as rubes. As he spoke the crowd got all riled up, booed and hollered. I could almost see something taking hold of them, something I hadn't noticed at other political rallies. You could feel the anger, fear, and division. You could almost smell the hate. And this was supposed to be a room full of Christians.

Of course, I didn't necessarily disagree with this operative's political ideas, or with the fact that our nation's capital is full of politicians we ought to run out of town on a rail. But I knew the truth of the matter, too: Political solutions wouldn't fix our country's problems. Political solutions wouldn't fix our division, hatred, or anger. So I took the stage, and I did what I do. I offered the crowd a spiritual solution. I told them the government could never provide the kind of health care they needed—the eternal kind. I told them they should invest in the only thing that'd give them the hope of eternal resurrection from the grave—the gospel story of Jesus. Then I pointed to the divisions in America, how we'd been given over to a depraved mind, how we seem to do all the things we ought not do according to Scripture. I told them we needed to get out and vote for godly people in America, people who could bring us together under godly principles like the Ten Commandments. When I said my piece, I got off the stage.

In the days after that rally, I sat in my recliner and pondered that event. The crowd was frenzied, divided. And it wasn't the kind of division Jesus said would result from the preaching of the gospel. It was a different kind. A vitriolic, worldly division. It was the sort of division I'd rather not be associated with, which raised the question: In their anger and fear, did that crowd hear a word I'd said about Christ, about eternal health care, about the importance of a system of laws founded on the Bible?

I doubted it.

The anger and fear, the name-calling and division spun up by so many politicians these days is not one-sided. Conservatives fall prey to it. Liberals fall prey to it. And insult by insult, brick by brick, we've built a strong and mighty wall between the two sides. Each stands on its respective side (left-winger or right-winger) and lobs grenades over to the other side. With that wall firmly in place, unity has become a pipe dream.

But here's what I know from experience: walls can come down. Divisions can be repaired. Unity is possible through the saving message of Christ. How do I know? I've experienced it.

The gospel of Jesus found me when I was as poor as dirt and as redneck as they come. (For the record, only one of those things has changed.) Before my conversion to Christ, I didn't have a moral fiber in my body. I didn't run with business leaders or upstanding men of the community. I might not have known a single person who owned a suit. I consorted with one type of person—poor, hell-raising, duck-hunting, deer-poaching rednecks. What'd we think of those slick-suited business types who were different from us? Not much.

When I came into the church, everything changed. I still had my fair share of redneck friends, folks who lived on the blue-collar side of the tracks. But as I started attending Bible studies and church services, I started meeting folks from different socio-economic classes. I met folks who were deadly serious about politics and those who weren't. I spent more time with bankers and business owners. And though I'd always known my fair share of African American folks—as a youngster, I'd picked cotton with many—this was the first time I was rubbing shoulders with them in the church congregation.

There, under the preaching of Bill Smith at the White's Ferry Road Church, I learned this truth of the gospel: in the family of God, there was no distinction between the sons and daughters of the Almighty. We were all equal. I might be a river rat. The man on my left might be a black factory worker. The fella to my right might be a white, suit-wearing banker. The woman in front of me might be a stay-at-home mom or a saleswoman or an attorney. We might have various political views (although the Bible calls us to agree on things like abortion and marriage). Under the gospel of Jesus, we'd been made part of the same family, Bill said. No one was more favored than any other.

This unifying message wasn't just talk at White's Ferry Road Church. The congregation took it as the gospel truth. There wasn't any pressure to gussy up, to go out and buy some new suit or expensive church clothes. They didn't ask me to shave my beard or clean up. They didn't ask me to adopt a certain political party or ideology. They took me as I was, scruffy and unshorn, sometimes a little odiferous, depending on whether I'd had chores to do that morning.

Don't get me wrong; we weren't perfect. Over the years a few folks at the church have lost sight of the truth. They've suggested it might be good for some of us to shave our beards or dress up or be a little less vocal about our personal political positions. Time after time, though, we manage to come back to the truth of the gospel. The Almighty looks at the heart, and he wants us to be unified under his saving message. Couldn't our modern world use a dose of this message of unity?

America is divided. Even a C+ man like me can see as much.

We divide along political lines. (Are you a Republican or Democrat?)

We point out the different economic classes. (Are you working class or a white-collar fella?)

We increasingly divide along racial and gender lines. (Do I even need to explain that one?)

There doesn't seem to be any common ground these days. Instead of peace and harmony, there's nothing but discord, division, and protest. There's racial violence, and class warfare, and gender strife. We're yard dogs, all at each other's throats.

When the Founding Fathers set the stakes of America, they envisioned something less divided, something more unified. They envisioned a society where men and women came together under a single truth. They memorialized this truth in the Declaration of Independence, writing:

> We hold these truths to be self-evident, that all men are cre-
> ated equal, that they are endowed by their Creator with certain
> unalienable Rights, that among these are Life, Liberty and the
> Pursuit of Happiness.

The founding ideal of America was that the very real and living God had made all men the same, and he wanted us to be free. He wanted us to share rights, to be unified under his truth, and to be happy, happy, happy.

There's no doubt that our forefathers didn't follow this ideal perfectly, especially in their enactment of laws. As I wrote in chapter 7, they didn't end slavery when they declared independence, and they participated in a land grab from the Native Americans. They had different ideas of what *liberty* meant, too, and they divided into political parties almost as soon as the country was founded. But still, from the very beginning, they hoped for a society that would be unified under the principles in the Declaration of Independence. They hoped for a country where folks worked together to build an equal, virtuous, and ultimately prosperous society.

How'd we get derailed? The enemy, the father of lies, sneaked in and told us this whopper: unity is not possible. All people are not created equal, he said. He's preyed on our differences—religious, political, economic, racial, and gender. He's made us believe that true equality is impossible, convinced us that the only way to get what we deserve is to divide and conquer. And in pointing out our divisions, the enemy of our souls and our country has sowed the seeds of chaos, violence, and even murder.

Consider the divisions of the last ten years. We've had the Occupy Wall Street movement, where the young and unemployed protested the rich and powerful. Racial tensions built until Ferguson, Missouri, blew up, and how many racially motivated protests have we seen since? Most disturbing, we've seen neo-Nazi groups cropping up across America in the last couple of years, and they make no bones about reestablishing white supremacy, the original sin of America.

The enemy of our country's soul has come to steal, kill, and destroy everything our Founding Fathers stood for, and he's done it through division. And if it's true that God is dead, is there any unifying force that can help bridge these divisions? Will secular humanists bridge the division? They haven't yet.

There's a simple solution to all our disunity, and it's a truth found in the absolute truth of God's Word. We can return to the Almighty and understand how he's created us to be unified under his message. What is that message? That all of us are created in the image of God, and so he loves us all without distinction.

Jesus came preaching the unifying love of God. But he didn't just preach it. He embodied it. He spent time with men and women, rich and poor, sick and healthy, Jews and Gentiles. He asked a Roman employee—Matthew, the tax collector—to become his disciple. He also asked a Jewish zealot who would have hated that Roman tax collector—Peter—to follow along. He touched the lepers (Matt. 8:2–3). He spent time with the hated Samaritans, including a second-class, outcast, divorced-five-times-over Samaritan woman (John 4:1–42). Jesus came, and he showed no favoritism, only love for all.

To remove any doubt about the law of impartial love, Jesus made himself clear. In the book of Luke, a lawyer asked Jesus how he might inherit eternal life. Jesus flipped the question around and asked what the Scriptures had to say on the matter. The lawyer responded by quoting the law, and said, "'Love the Lord your God with all your heart with all your soul and with all your strength and with all your mind;' and 'Love your neighbor as yourself'" (10:27). After Jesus agreed with his answer, the lawyer asked, "And who is my neighbor?" (v. 29).

Lawyers—always splitting hairs.

The question led Jesus to his clearest teaching on equality and unity, and he did it all through a parable. You may recall it. A Jewish man was on his way to Jerusalem when he was attacked by robbers, Jesus said. Left on the road for dead, the man was in dire need of help. A Jewish priest happened past him on the road, but he didn't stop to help. Instead, he crossed to the other side of the road. A Levite—another devoted Jewish man—likewise refused to help him and crossed to the other side of the road. But then a Samaritan, a man despised by the Jews, passed by and helped the beaten and bloody man. He bandaged his wounds and gave him a drink. He then took him to a local inn and left money for the owner so that the man would be taken care of.

Jesus finished the parable and then asked the lawyer, "Which of these three do you think was a neighbor to the man who fell into the hands of the robbers?"

"The one who had mercy on him," he said of the Samaritan.

"Go and do likewise," Jesus said (vv. 25–37).

Jesus' teaching through this parable was simple. All people are our neighbors, even those of different nationalities or ethnicities. Even those of different political beliefs, just like the Jew and Samaritan. Even those whom we might consider our enemies. And how are we to treat those neighbors, those we see as different? We're to treat them just as we would want to be treated—with self-sacrificing love.

Jesus came to destroy the divisions between men, to bring all of us into the family of everlasting life. After his death, burial, resurrection, and ascension, he sent the Spirit of the Almighty on the disciples, and through that Spirit, he showed them just how he intended to bring people of all makes and models into the fold.

After Jesus ascended to heaven, the apostles were gathered together in a room in Jerusalem, trying to sort out what came next. That's when something unexpected happened. A sound like a rushing wind blew through the room, the Holy Spirit fell on the disciples, and they began sharing the good news of Jesus in different languages. The writer of Acts recorded what happened next:

When the day of Pentecost came . . . there were staying in Jerusalem God-fearing Jews from every nation under heaven. When they heard this sound, a crowd came together in bewilderment, because each one heard their own language being spoken. Utterly amazed, they asked: "Aren't all these who are speaking Galileans? Then how is it that each of us hears them in our native language? Parthians, Medes and Elamites; residents of Mesopotamia, Judea and Cappadocia, Pontus and Asia, Phrygia and Pamphylia, Egypt and the parts of Libya near Cyrene; visitors from Rome (both Jews and converts to Judaism); Cretans and Arabs—we hear them declaring the wonders of God in our own tongues!" Amazed and perplexed, they asked one another, "What does this mean?" (2:1, 5–12)

Peter heard the people, and he answered:

"Fellow Jews and all of you who live in Jerusalem, let me explain this to you. . . . This is what was spoken by the prophet Joel: 'In the last days, God says, I will pour out my Spirit on all people.'" (2:14, 16–17)

Under the influence of the Holy Spirit, Peter spoke the two words that would convey the unifying truth of the gospel to a very diverse crowd: *all people*. The Spirit of God had made a way for all nationalities, and though the early spread of the gospel was only to the Jews from other nations, it would soon spread to the Gentiles.

After the establishment of the church at Pentecost, the Almighty expanded his message. Coming to Peter in a dream, God made it clear: his gospel message was not just for the Jews; it was for everyone. In that dream the Almighty told Peter that men were coming to visit, men who were servants of a Gentile centurion named Cornelius. Cornelius was a different nationality, came from a different religious background, and most certainly had different politics than Peter. Still, God made it clear to Peter. "Do not hesitate to go with them," the Almighty said, "for I have sent them" (Acts 10:20).

Sure enough, the servants came, and following the Word of the Almighty that'd come to him, Peter followed them. He made his way to Cornelius's house, and he shared the good news of equality and unity.

> "You are well aware that it is against our law for a Jew to associate with or visit a Gentile. But God has shown me that I should not call anyone impure or unclean. . . . I now realize how true it is that God does not show favoritism but accepts from every nation the one who fears him and does what is right." (vv. 28, 34–35)

Peter continued, presenting the gospel message to Cornelius, and the Holy Spirit fell on the entire household. Peter baptized them on the spot, and that baptism changed the face of the church forever. From that moment on, it was apparent. Christ made no distinction between people. (As a Gentile from Louisiana, I'm most grateful for Peter's dream.)

The message of divine equality would pass to Paul after his conversion too. Before he was struck down by the Almighty on the road to Damascus and converted, Paul was one of the Jewish religious leaders of the day. He firmly believed the Jewish people were God's most favored folks, and he wouldn't have entertained the idea that the Almighty cared a lick about the Gentiles. After his conversion, though, he came to understand the unifying truth of the gospel, and he preached that message everywhere he went.

During his second missionary journey—a missionary trip that led him to the Gentiles in Asia, Macedonia, and Greece—Paul made a pit stop in Athens. There he visited Mars Hill, a place where folks from around the world gathered to discuss the religious ideas of the day. On that hill Paul preached his most famous sermon, proclaiming that God's message was for everyone, even the Gentiles. He preached, "From one man [God] made all the nations, that they should inhabit the whole earth. . . . As some of your own poets have said, 'We are his offspring'" (Acts 17:26, 28). Paul then told the people gathered on that hill to repent because the judgment was coming through Jesus, the man God had raised from the dead. The writer of Acts recorded that when they heard of the coming judgment, of the escape from that judgment provided by Jesus, some became followers of Paul and believed. What's more, the writer of Acts made it clear that both a man, Dionysius, and a woman, Damaris, followed Paul's teaching.

See? God calls all sorts of people, and Paul continued to make this clear in his writings to the church. To the Roman church he wrote that God's message was for the Jews and Gentiles alike because, "God does not show favoritism" (Rom. 2:11). To the Galatians Paul wrote that among the believers, "there is neither Jew nor Gentile, neither slave nor free, nor is there male and female, for you are all one in Christ Jesus" (Gal. 3:28). To the slave owners in Ephesus, he wrote, "Do not threaten [your slaves], since you know that he who is both their Master and yours is in heaven, and there is no favoritism with him" (Eph. 6:9). And for those of you who might think I'm saying Paul affirmed slavery, think again. In fact, if the slave owners of the day had taken his teaching to its logical conclusion, I think they'd have set their subjects free.

It wasn't just Peter and Paul who preached this unifying message of truth to all nations. While in exile on the island of Patmos, John, the beloved disciple of Jesus, had a vision of the end times. John recorded this scene from that revelation:

Then I saw another angel flying in midair, and he had the eternal gospel to proclaim to those who live on the earth—to every nation, tribe, language and people. He said in a loud voice, "Fear God and give him glory, because the hour of his judgment has come. Worship him who made the heavens, the earth, the sea and the springs of water." (Rev. 14:6–7)

Every nation, tribe, language, and people come together under the gospel. Could there be a more unifying message?

The gospel of equality isn't just about nationality, ethnicity, and political affiliation. It applies all the way down the line, even to economic status. James, the brother of Jesus, addressed making distinctions in worship services based on economic status. After he warned the church against showing favoritism in worship, he wrote,

> Suppose a man comes into your meeting wearing a gold ring and fine clothes, and a poor man in filthy old clothes also comes in. If you show special attention to the man wearing fine clothes and say, 'Here's a good seat for you,' but say to the poor man, 'You stand there' or 'Sit on the floor by my feet,' have you not discriminated among yourselves and become judges with evil thoughts? (James 2:2–4)

Judges with evil thoughts—those are some strong words.

Why was it so evil to distinguish between the rich and poor in the worship service? James answered that question with a question, writing, "Has not God chosen those who are poor in the eyes of the world to be rich in faith and to inherit the kingdom he promised those who love him?" (v. 5). James thought it was clear—the only savings account the Almighty cares about is the savings account of faith. So, instead of honoring one's material wealth, the church should honor the riches of faithfulness.

The truth is the truth, no matter how you cut it, and the truth is, the church should be the most unified place in all of America.

We shouldn't tolerate division. The other truth is this: the lie of the evil one has crept into the church. Just as he's convinced the world that unity isn't possible, hasn't he convinced us too? Isn't the American church just as divided as the rest of the world? Do we look any different?

You could look at the churches in Northern Louisiana alone and see just how divided we are. There are white churches and black churches, rich churches and poor churches, conservative churches and liberal churches. And even within those churches, aren't distinctions made? Aren't the well-dressed or rich given positions of authority or placed on committees or given recognition while the less wealthy find themselves sitting on the back pews? Don't we show special attention to the man or woman wearing fine clothes? And how well do we listen to the faithful in raggedy T-shirts and camo and beards that stretch to midchest?

Be honest.

The truth hurts, don't it?

To the outside observer, the person who hasn't accepted the good news of Jesus, I suspect they don't see us as any more unified than the rest of the world. That leads me to this conclusion: the people who claim to follow the Almighty don't. Instead, we've believed the lie of the enemy too.

I'm not the sort of fella who sees demons around every corner or attributes every weird or wild occurrence to demonic possession.

That said, when I've seen it, it's been unmistakable. On the few occasions when I've seen possession of biblical proportions, it's been accompanied by vile name-calling, hate, and the worst kind of divisiveness.

At White's Ferry Road Church, we have the opportunity to work with our fair share of rehab patients. They go in for alcohol or drugs, and we tag along and share the good news of Jesus. Years ago I made just such a visit to a rehab facility, and no sooner had I stepped into the building, a patient met me and went on a tirade before I even spoke a word. She called me a Bible thumper, told me my religion and politics weren't welcome in the place. She hollered and yelled and cussed at me. As she was getting me down the road, I turned to Ephesians 4:26 and quoted the Scriptures over her holler'n. "In your anger do not sin," I shouted, which only made her angrier, and she stormed out of the room.

The receptionist saw the entire exchange, and she stopped by to make sure I wasn't bothered. I told her I wasn't and asked whether I could sit with this woman who'd called me every name under the sun. The woman cocked her head and said, "Sure, but good luck."

We waited in the lobby, and after a few minutes, the patient returned, cursing up a storm. I waited her out, and when she was finished, said, "I can't help you if you don't listen." I reckon I struck the right tone, because she calmed a little, sat in the chair across from me, and then asked, "What'dya got?"

I gave the woman the good news of Jesus, started with her sin and showed how she'd come under the influence of the evil one. Hatred, malice, name-calling, cursing—these were all tools of the evil one to separate us from the saving message of Jesus, I told her, but there was good news. I didn't get to the good news, though, because the woman slammed her head on the table and made a low gurgle like something was stuck in the back of her throat. She stood, turned, and began to run toward the bathroom, but she didn't make it. She projectile vomited across the room, then ran to the bathroom, slammed and locked the door. After a few minutes she came out, cleaned-up and quieter.

"Can y'all help me?" she begged.

"Jesus can help anyone who calls on his name," I said.

I shared the good news of Jesus, how he'd come to free us from the enemy's grip. I told her that all her sins could be forgiven and that she could have eternal life. She didn't have to see me as her enemy, I said, and she could join my family, the family of God. She listened, silent as a stump, then asked if she could think on the message I shared and asked whether I might come back the next day. I agreed, and she thanked me for my time.

I showed up the next day around the same time, and there she was. She was clean-faced and smiling. She didn't call me a single name. She didn't spew the first curse word. She asked if I'd take her to the river that ran past the facility and baptize her, and that's just what I did. I raised her from the waters, and the woman who'd hated me the day before for my religion and politics was now my sister in Christ. She hugged me, then walked out of the water and back toward the facility.

Before I left, the receptionist found me and told me she thought it was nothing short of a miracle. It was a demonic deliverance, she said. Looking back on it, I suppose she was right. The enemy of the Almighty thought anger, hatred, name-calling, and divisive cursing could drive me away from that girl who needed nothing more than Jesus. He thought he could divide us and conquer her soul. But the lies of the enemy are no match for the unifying truth of God.

The good news of the gospel is that it frees us from the lies (and possession) of the enemy. It can bring ultimate unity, if only we believe it. The gospel turns conservative redneck duck hunters and hate-filled rehab patients into family. It brings together folks of every ethnicity, nationality, economic class, and gender. It heals the division in our country. It might even save that man who spewed anger, malice, and division at the political event, if only he'd trust it.

American church, look around. Our country is more divided than ever. But we have the solution, the greatest tool for freeing the world of the lie. We have the Word of Truth. It's the tool that might tear down the wall that already exists in our country. It's the tool that might make a family of us again. So let's get back to it. When we gather on Sunday mornings, let's model a love for our neighbors that shows no favoritism based on class, color, or nationality. But let's not stop there. Let's be examples to the rest of the world. Let's carry the truth of Christ's unity out into the workplace, into public schools, into the rehab centers. Let's carry it into the political process, into the voter booth. Let's share it with those who are possessed by their father, the evil one, and let's watch deliverance happen.

And this, I suppose, brings me to the most important point of the book: church, it's time to go out and be the church.

THE LIE: CHURCH PARTICIPATION AND DAY-TO-DAY LIFE SHOULD BE KEPT SEPARATE.

THE TRUTH: THE CHURCH IS GOD'S PRESENCE IN THE DAY-TO-DAY WORLD, KEEPING THE WORLD FROM BECOMING HELL ON EARTH.

In the early days Duck Commander wasn't a cash cow. I worked hard and did the best I could, but in the end there wasn't much to show for it. In the first year I generated chicken scratch—$8,200 in sales, which didn't leave a whole lot for a family of five to live on. But I was faithful and committed to the vision, and the following year the business generated $13,000 in sales. In the third year sales increased to $22,000, and in the fourth year to $37,000. By the early 2000s Duck Commander had become a thriving business, one that supported my family in addition to the families of a few employees. We had sold duck calls to stores throughout the country and growth opportunities were multiplying.

As Duck Commander grew I traveled more and more. Outspoken about my faith as I was, I visited my fair share of church events across the country. It wasn't just church events though. I also traveled across the country and spoke at sporting goods store events and hunting conventions. Whenever I went out, I'd demonstrate the superiority of the Duck Commander calls. I'd show the attendees how to use the calls to command ducks to their blinds, and time after time the old boys would tell me just how much my calls sounded like real ducks. As much of a privilege as that was, the calls were of secondary importance to me. What was my primary goal? To share the life-saving message of Jesus. And if the duck calls drew a larger crowd to hear that message, it was all the better.

Just before the launch of *Duck Dynasty*, I attended the opening of some big-box sporting goods store in Minnesota. When it was my turn, the manager welcomed me to the stage, which had been set up in the middle of the store. I walked to the podium and surveyed the crowd that'd gathered, most of whom looked like my kind of folks—hunters, fishermen, and trappers who wore camouflage and sported ample facial hair. I pulled my duck calls from my bag and performed my usual calling routine under that red, white, and blue banner. Then, after giving what I believed to be a rousing presentation, I put the calls back into my bag and pulled out my Bible.

"Minnesota," I said, holding up the Good Book, "let me tell you about something more important than mallard calls."

I shared the good news of Jesus with those old boys, how he'd come making promises. He said he'd remove all our sins—past, present, and future. He said he'd free us from guilt and shame. He promised he'd raise our bodies from the grave. He'd give us a new and everlasting life, and if we follow his truth in this life, we'd be freed from the very real consequences of chasing after our sinful and lawless desires.

"Listen," I said as I closed my presentation, "I've tried the other way of living, including living under the rule of the king of beers. Let me tell you something gentlemen: Following Jesus? It's the only way to roll."

With that, I exited the stage, made my way to the airport, and returned to Louisiana.

It was an engagement much like any other, and truth was, I didn't think much about it after the fact. That is, until about five years later when Miss Kay came into the living room carrying a letter. "You need to read this," she said, and she handed me the already opened envelope. It was from a name I didn't recognize, and the return address was from Minnesota. I'm not one for fan mail, but because Miss Kay told me I needed to read it, I unfolded the letter and went to town.

It was a long letter, five pages to be exact, and it was from a man who'd attended the big-box store opening all those years ago. It didn't begin with the usual fan mail tone, but instead opened with a three-page tirade about how offended the writer had been by my gospel presentation. He told me he left the store disgusted. He said that in the years that followed, he'd made it his life's goal to dog-cuss me to anyone who'd listen. He ripped me to shreds everywhere he went and told his friends and family he'd never blow a Duck Commander call because I'd mixed business and religion. What's more, he asked his friends and family to join in his boycott of Duck Commander products. He was a regular anti-Phil apologist, he said, and his sentiment toward me rose to the level of hate.

But then, after years of living in all that hatred, something shifted.

About four years into his personal vendetta, the old boy was mulling over how much he hated me, and as he did, he considered his life. It was a real mess, marked by anger, addiction, and the consequences of chasing after sin. In considering his life, he'd reexamined my message. I'd told him he was a sinner, sure. I'd told him of the dire earthly consequences of that sin, consequences he knew all too well. I'd also told him of the eternal consequence, of everlasting death. But hadn't I also given him the solution to his problem? Hadn't I told him how he could receive forgiveness of his sins and the promise of a new life? Hadn't I told him how he could escape the hell of his own anger and find the rarest commodity of life—peace of mind? Hadn't I told him how he could beat the grave? He took stock of the message and came to a simple conclusion: I'd offered him the best news he'd ever heard, and he'd gone out of his way to hate me for it.

There in his living room, he wrote, he gave his life to Christ. He'd been baptized and had been living in the truth for more than a year. Everything I'd promised—freedom from his personal hell and peace of mind—he'd found to be true, and he shared the message everywhere he went. He'd even reversed his boycott and had become an apologist for all things Duck Commander and *Duck Dynasty*. Now he was writing a letter to apologize.

I folded up the letter, put it back in the envelope, and gave thanks for my new brother in Minnesota. He didn't need to apologize, of course. He'd never really hurt me in the first place. After all, I'd only done what I was instructed to do—go into the world preaching the good news and making disciples. Even though the man thought he hated me for all those years, he'd really hated the message of Christ. But thanks to the Almighty, he'd come to know the truth, and the truth had set him free from all that hate. Now he worshiped everywhere he went.

This is what the truth does, see. It sets us free from sin, free to worship.

As believers in Jesus, as members of the church, we have access to the ultimate truth: God is alive and active, and he wants to save us from the hell of our own anger, hatred, and sin. He wants to save us from actual hell too. It's the most powerful truth there is, the truth that might save the soul of America from the devastating consequences of sin. If this truth is so powerful, why doesn't it seem to be taking hold? Why does it seem that the powerful message of the gospel is absent in the world around us?

As much as it pains me to say it, I think the answer is plain. The church has forgotten its purpose, forgotten that we're supposed to be carrying the truth of the Almighty out to the world. Instead, we've hidden our message under a bushel. We've kept our message locked up in a two-hour Sunday morning service and gone along with the rest of the world during the other 166 hours of the week.

The people of God—the very mouthpieces of Christ himself—have forgotten the essence of true worship. Is it any wonder we've lost so much ground in America?

There's a lot of talk these days about the drop-off in church attendance. The news outlets point to the decline in church growth.[1] The implication? God must be dead. People are leaving, they say, and so the message of the church must be irrelevant for modern America.

And you know the saddest part? We're the ones who've taught the world that the church is irrelevant.

Outside of the Sunday church services, are our lives all that different? Some studies show that 80 percent of Christians between the ages of eighteen and twenty-nine have premarital sex.[2] By some estimates Christians account for more than 50 percent of abortions in America.[3] Some reports show that 64 percent of Christian men and 15 percent of Christian women are addicted to pornography.[4] The difference in divorce rates between Christians and non-Christians is negligible. And look around you: think American Christians are just as greedy, arrogant, and insolent as the rest of the world? You bet we are.

I've identified the problem, see, and the problem is us.

Over the last fifty years, the American church has been a dismal failure. Instead of trying to carry the truth of the Almighty out to the world, instead of sharing his love, we've created comfortable Christian communities where our faith is rarely tested. We gather together in multi-million-dollar facilities with comfortable stadium seating, concert-worthy sound systems, and laser light shows. We create experiences that are supposed to be relevant, rock shows that sound just like the music of the world. And as we've retreated to these places, these experiences, we've withdrawn from government, allowed our faith to be squeezed out of public schools, let our voices be silenced in the workplace. See? Under pressure of the advancing secular age, we retreated to our church buildings as society around us descended into godless chaos.

In this book I've outlined the lies the evil one has used to steal, kill, and destroy the soul of America. Of all the lies, perhaps the worst is the one he's peddled to the church, the one we've bought hook, line, and sinker: church is an activity we attend two hours a week, and our faith is to be expressed there, not out in the world. Why is this lie the worst of the lot? Because we, the people of God, should know better.

Jesus never meant for his message to be contained within a building or confined to a service. He came to seek and save the lost, and where were the lost? They were out in the streets. The lost were the everyday businessmen, the fishermen, the women working at home. The lost were the children running through the streets. The lost were the beggars, the crippled, and the leprous. They were the tax collectors, prostitutes, and sinners. So, although Jesus preached from time to time in the synagogue, he spent most of his time spreading his good news where the people were—in the world. In fact, Jesus was among the people so much that the religious teachers of the day took issue with it. They asked why he spent so much time with tax collectors and sinners. They called him a drunkard because he attended parties where sinners were. They watched as he spent time with women—women with bad reputations at that. Time and time again, they took issue with just how *in the world* Jesus was. But as Jesus went, he wasn't compartmentalizing his faith. He was out there preaching. And what was he preaching? Freedom.

Freedom from sin.

Freedom from death.

Freedom from religious obligation.

Freedom to worship the Almighty everywhere, all the time.

Take, for example, the story John told us in the fourth chapter of his gospel. After traveling throughout the region, Jesus and his disciples took a break in a backwater Samaritan town. Sitting by the town well, Jesus sent the disciples into town to buy food. While he waited, a Samaritan woman came to draw water, and Jesus struck up a conversation with her. Getting to the point, as Jesus was prone to do, he shared with her the best news—that he could satisfy her spiritual thirst. He also told her he knew everything about her life of sin, the way she'd cycled through husbands and how she was currently living with a man who wasn't her husband. The woman was astounded and said, "Sir . . . I can see that you are a prophet" (4:19).

No kidding, gal!

Thinking Jesus might be able to answer the age-old Samaritan question of worship, she pointed up to the mountain across the way. "Our ancestors worshiped on this mountain," she said, "but you Jews claim that the place where we must worship is in Jerusalem" (v. 20).

It was a statement, but it carried an implied question. *Where am I supposed to worship the Almighty?* Jesus came to destroy the barrier between the temple and the streets, and his answer must have surprised her. He said,

"A time is coming when you will worship the Father neither on this mountain nor in Jerusalem. . . . A time is coming and has now come when the true worshipers will worship the Father in the Spirit and in truth, for they are the kind of worshipers the Father seeks. God is spirit, and his worshipers must worship in the Spirit and in truth" (vv. 21–24).

Jesus couldn't have been any clearer. Worship of the Almighty wasn't meant to be hidden away within the four walls of a building. It wasn't meant to be compartmentalized or kept out of society. True worship—proclaiming God's glory and truth—happens everywhere the Christian goes. Why? Because the Christian is the very temple of the Almighty's Spirit.

Time and time again, Jesus showed the disciples how to carry the good news out to the dying world. They followed him from town to town as he preached forgiveness of sins, healed the sick, and performed miracles. They watched as he shared the truth around dinner tables. They were even sent out to the countryside to preach the good news to the people (Matt. 10; Luke 10). And after his resurrection from the dead, just before his ascension to the Father, he left his people with one parting instruction. "Go," he said, "and make disciples of all nations, baptizing them in the name of the Father and of the Son and of the Holy Spirit, and teaching them to obey everything I have commanded you" (Matt. 28:19–20).

Go.

Outside the four walls of any building.

Out into the world.

Out to the places where the people are.

Go to the public schools and places of employment and the voter booth. Go, go, go and mix it up with the people, sharing the absolute truth of the Almighty with grace. Sound scary to get out there and share the good news with a hostile world? Not to me. Why? Because Christ gave us this promise with his command to go: "Surely I am with you always, to the very end of the age" (v. 20).

Paul understood the commands of Jesus to worship in Spirit and truth, and in that worship, to carry the good news of the Almighty out to the world. In his letter to the Romans, Paul made clear that simply participating in a temple service was not "worship." Though attending a service may be a part of worship, Paul saw worship as a full-body experience, something that happens wherever believers go. In the letter to the Romans, he put it this way:

> Therefore, I urge you, brothers and sisters, in view of God's mercy, to offer your bodies as a living sacrifice, holy and pleasing to God—this is your true and proper worship. Do not conform to the pattern of this world, but be transformed by the renewing of your mind. (12:1–2)

According to Paul, true worship means living our daily lives as a sacrifice for the world around us. How do we do that? We don't operate by the world's agenda. We operate differently. "Keep your spiritual fervor," Paul wrote, "serving the Lord. Be joyful in hope, patient in affliction, faithful in prayer. Share with the Lord's people who are in need. Practice hospitality" (vv. 11–13).

Paul wrote that our worship is best expressed as we *go*. It is expressed best as we carry the good news of Jesus outside the walls of our churches and into the chaotic, dying world. It's expressed through our acts of service, hospitality, prayer, and hope. It's expressed by being *different* from the world. But how will the world see that difference if we're not actually out in the world? How do we serve the Lord's agenda if we hide within a church building? We don't.

In his letter to the Ephesians, Paul reminded the people that God no longer lives in temples. Instead, he wrote that the people of the church "are being built together to become a dwelling in which God lives by his Spirit" (2:22). And as that dwelling place, it's our job to carry his message to the world, so that "through the church, the manifold wisdom of God should be made known to the rulers and authorities in the heavenly realms, according to his eternal purpose that he accomplished in Christ Jesus our Lord" (3:10–11). What's more, Paul recognized that as the church proclaimed the wisdom of God to the world and to the rulers and authorities in the heavenly realms, they would face opposition. So, he warned the people of God to "take [a] stand against the devil's schemes" and to prepare for a fight (6:11–12). In Ephesians 6:13–17 he wrote,

> Therefore put on the full armor of God, so that when the day of evil comes, you may be able to stand your ground, and after you have done everything, to stand. Stand firm then, with the belt of truth buckled around your waist, with the breastplate of righteousness in place, and with your feet fitted with the readiness that comes from the gospel of peace. In addition to all this, take up the shield of faith, with which you can extinguish all the flaming arrows of the evil one. Take the helmet of salvation and the sword of the Spirit, which is the word of God.

That passage begs a question, doesn't it? If our message was meant to stay cooped up in the walls of a building, who would need armor?

As we've explored throughout this book, the world around us is falling under the influence of the evil one. America has given itself to his delusions and has found itself mired in violence and chaos. It lacks peace. It's swimming in a cesspool of sexual desire. Yes, it is a virtual hell on earth here in America, but there's good news: Jesus came to save America from its wickedness, and he's chosen us, the church, to be the vehicle for that message. He's chosen us to be his very presence in the world, to push back the darkness around us with the light of his love.

American church, listen up: We are a collection of mobile homes for the Almighty. We carry his truth wherever we go. If you're a member of the church, it's time to stop hiding in the safety of your worship services. It's time to go out into the world and be the church, to live its mission out loud.

In the voting booth.

In the public schools.

In the workplace.

Wherever you are, you are the church, a vehicle for the good news of Jesus.

The truth set me free, and when it did, I received clear orders from headquarters: be a temple for the Almighty, and carry his truth with me everywhere I go. Preach. Baptize. Mix it up. So that's exactly what I did.

How?

I preached the gospel until folks were sick of hearing it. I also did my best to live a life of difference, to not be given to the things the Almighty hates—drunkenness, sexual immorality, greed, hatred. Miss Kay and I also did what we could to serve those around us, and we gave sacrificially from our resources, even when we were poor. We opened our home in hospitality to others, and as we did, we shared how all our gifts had come from the Almighty. We offered our bodies, our time, our talents, and our resources as sacrifices of worship, no matter where we were. This sort of worship—the daily kind—is the "Spirit and truth" kind of worship Christ wants from the lives of the believer, and the results speak for themselves.

As I've carried the truth of Jesus outside the four walls of the Sunday church meeting, I've piqued more than a little curiosity. Whether through *Duck Dynasty*, speaking events, or business engagements, folks have come to know of my commitment to the Almighty, and on more than one occasion, these folks—rich, poor, white, black, straight, gay—have sought me out as they've searched for their own answers to life. The stories are almost endless and they run the gamut. I've had world-renowned news anchors keep me on the line after interviews, to ask me if I could share the message of Jesus with them. I've shared the message with countless politicians, and many have told me they'd never heard the good news of Jesus, even though they'd been raised in church. I've never shied away from presenting the gospel to a celebrity, television personality, or corporate executive.

And as I've already mentioned, I shared the good news of Jesus with the president himself. (Mr. Trump, my offer to baptize you into Christ still stands. You ready to move on it?) On occasion, these VIPs have trusted in the gospel, but more often than not, the world's elites let the message pass right on by. And who knows? Maybe these folks are like that ol' boy from Minnesota: maybe it'll take them five years to move on it. But for every story I have of sharing the gospel with the rich and famous, there are countless others, stories of ordinary folks who make their way to the Louisiana river bottoms to ask an old river rat about the hope of Jesus. And these common folks? They're more prone to move on the good news.

I couldn't say how many folks have dropped in on Miss Kay and me unannounced over the years. It's certainly been hundreds, if not thousands. They come from all over the country, sometimes in beat-up pickup trucks or backfiring rust buckets. No matter how they come, Miss Kay and I welcome them in, and I give them a double-barrel helping of the truth.

I remember the time a young redneck, his girlfriend, mother, and a dozen of their friends came knocking a few years back. The crew had driven some distance to meet me and Miss Kay, and so we welcomed them into our home. As they sat in our living room, it became apparent that the young man and his lady weren't living in Christian purity, that they were shacking up. I looked at the old boy and asked him straight.

"Y'all aren't married, are you?"

"No," he said.

"And let me guess: you've been getting into her britches, haven't you?"

His face turned red, and he nodded.

"The Bible calls that sin," I said, "but let me tell you the good news of the One who can forgive all your sins, raise you to new life, and solve your biggest problem—death."

The boy and his girlfriend listened to my gospel presentation, and like so many others, they were taken with it. After I'd finished my spiel, I asked whether they wanted to move on the message, and they all but jumped at the chance and ran out the door toward the river. Just below my house, while the boy's mama and his group of friends watched, I lowered the two into the waters of baptism. As I raised the boy out of the water, I told him he was a new creature.

"This means you can't go back to shacking up with that pretty young girl till you're married." I said. "Understand?"

He didn't answer, didn't nod his head. He just smiled, then made a beeline to his girlfriend. There, on the banks of the Ouachita, he dropped to one knee and asked her to marry him. He turned to me and told me that the two of them were going to stop by the justice of the peace on the way out of town and make it official.

"I can make a phone call and get a wedding license," I said. "We can make it official right here."

He agreed, and as his mama was beaming from ear to ear, I nudged her and said, "Now we're getting somewhere."

This is just one example of what can happen when we offer ourselves as sacrifices of worship to the Almighty. He'll use us to bring the good news of Jesus to a world stuck in its own sin. He'll use us to bring freedom and peace of mind. He'll use us to change America, person by person, life by life, soul by soul. And as that happens, the very soul of America will be transformed.

Christ is the hope for a lost world, a world that will never darken the doors of the church. And if enough of us take our mission seriously, if we refuse to believe the lie that we should keep our faith confined to a two-hour church service, we might make a dent in this godless country. We might show the world that the Almighty isn't dead, that we haven't killed him at all. We might change the hearts of Americans and convince them of the other truths of Scripture: that there is an enemy who wants to steal their souls; that God alone is the Author of life; that sexuality was created for marriage; that God wants us to live lives of virtue; that the laws have been ordained to instruct us toward godliness; that the godly life strives for unity; and that the church is God's presence on earth. In short, we might keep America from becoming a living hell on earth.

So, here's the call, American church, and it's the same call Christ gave us on the mountain: get out of your structures; go into the world; carry the good news of Jesus as you go; preach the message in the voting booth, in the public schools, at your workplace; offer your homes, your hospitality, your homemade soup and corn bread to your unbelieving neighbors; make disciples; baptize; bring freedom to those who'll never darken the doors of the church. This is your very act of worship. This is what it means to be the church, Christ's presence to a dying world.

THE LIE: CHRISTIANS SHOULD
SHUT THEIR TRAPS.

THE TRUTH: GOD'S PEOPLE ARE HIS
PROPHETIC VOICE IN THE WORLD.

I was sitting in my living room—our home served as the Duck Commander office back in those days—when the phone rang.

"Hello. Duck Commander. This is Phil."

"I need to order some duck calls," the man on the other end of the phone said.

I asked him what he'd like, and he started in on his order. He started listing calls, and between each one, for whatever reason, he used the Lord's name in vain. Twice. Three times. The fourth time he used Jesus' name, I knew what I had to do. First: get his mailing address and credit card information. Next: ask him why he was so intent on cursing the Lord.

"Let me ask you something," I said after I'd written down his MasterCard number. "Why would you curse the only One who could save you from eternal death?"

There was nothing but silence on the other end of the line.

"You still there?"

He responded flatly, "Yeah, I'm still here, Hoss. You got my duck call order?"

"Yeah. I got it," I said.

The receiver slammed down on the other side, and I heard the dial tone.

Ten minutes passed, and the phone rang again.

"Hello. Duck Commander. This is Phil."

"It's me again," the familiar voice said.

"Well, what about it?" I said. "Why would you curse the only One who could save you from death? That's the question on the table."

There was another moment of silence, then he said, "I've never really thought about it."

"Well, you're going six feet deep one of these days," I said, "and you cannot escape it without divine intervention." I looked up the contact information from his order sheet and said, "You know what you ought to do? You ought to drive over to West Monroe from Decatur, Alabama, and let me tell you a story. When I'm finished, I bet you won't curse God anymore."

I reckon he took it as some sort of challenge, because he raised his voice and said, "Well, I might do that, Hoss!"

I raised my voice back, "Well, maybe you should, Hoss!" Then I hung up on him.

A week went by, and I was sitting in my recliner when I heard a knock at the door. I shouted at the door, told whomever it was to come on in, and a fella stepped into my living room, buddy in tow.

"You know who I am?" he asked. I told him I didn't know him from Adam, and with the straightest face, he said, "I'm that fella who was cursing God on the phone, and I ain't leaving until you tell me why I shouldn't."

"Well, friend, you have come to the right place," I said.

There in my living room, I told the two gentlemen the good news of Jesus. They listened closely, and about halfway through, then started bawling like little boys. I finished, then asked whether they'd like to go down to the river to be baptized. They didn't think twice, said they'd like to move on the good news before they made their way back to Decatur. So I took them down to the river, to the place I'd baptized so many people before, and buried them in the waters of baptism. When I raised them up, I asked whether they needed any dry clothes for their six-hour trip back to Decatur.

"No, sir," they said, smiling. "We're in good shape."

They jumped into their truck and drove back to Alabama, sopping wet.

Seventeen years later, I found myself in Decatur, Alabama, where I was scheduled to preach at a local church. Truth was, I'd baptized so many folks over the years that I hadn't thought twice about the old boy who'd once cursed God, then followed him. That is, until I was at dinner with the preacher that night.

While we were eating, one of the brothers at the table asked if I remembered so-and-so, a name I didn't recognize. I told him I didn't, and that's when he reminded me of the story.

"He was the ol' boy who'd cursed God while ordering some duck calls and you challenged him over it."

"Oh, yes. I remember now," I said. "The fella who drove all the way to Louisiana to be baptized?"

"That's the one," he said. "You should know that he came home after that meeting at your place, and he gave it to us real good for never sharing the gospel with him. He told us he shouldn't have had to drive all the way to Louisiana to find a man who'd challenge him on his sin and lead him into the truth."

"Whatever happened to him?" I asked.

"He's one of the leaders of this church now."

The man who'd used his freedom of speech to curse the Almighty now used it to preach his name, I was told. It was a modern-day Saul-to-Paul conversion story.

There is power in the gospel when it's preached. It sets people free. It changes folks' lives. It puts us on the path to everlasting life. But how in the world will people come to know this freedom if there aren't any preachers? And how can there be preachers if folks don't exercise their God-given and constitutionally recognized freedom of speech? Perhaps this is why free speech is under such attack in this day and age. Perhaps this is why Satan would have us believe the lie that Christians don't deserve the liberty to speak their minds.

The Founding Fathers knew the importance of individual liberties. They believed all Americans should enjoy the freedom to practice their religion, the freedom to gather together as people of faith, and the freedom to share what they believe through free speech. What's more, our forefathers believed these liberties were granted to all men by God as natural rights, rights that couldn't be taken away by any government. As Thomas Jefferson noted, "Can the liberties of a nation be secure when we have removed a conviction that these liberties are the gift of God?"[1]

Nope.

This being the case, they took measures to limit the government's interference with these liberties by including these words in the United States Constitution: "Congress shall make no law respecting an establishment of religion, or prohibiting the free exercise thereof; or abridging the freedom of speech."

In their infinite wisdom, our forefathers hoped to protect us from some future tyrannical government that might try to remove these liberties. They also knew that if individual liberties—liberties like the freedom of religion, of assembly, and property ownership—were to be scaled back, it would most likely start with the erosion of freedom of speech. In fact, Ben Franklin wrote, "The Security of Property, and the Freedom of Speech always go together; and in those wretched Countries where a Man cannot call his Tongue his own, he can scarce call any Thing else his own. Whoever would overthrow the Liberty of a Nation, must begin by subduing the Freeness of Speech."[2]

James Monroe, the fifth president of the United States, believed that freedom of speech was a fundamental hedge against tyranny. He wrote, "Of the liberty of conscience in matters of religious faith, of speech and of the press; of the trial by jury; . . . of the benefit of the writ of habeas corpus; of the right to keep and bear arms. . . . If these rights are . . . secured against encroachments, it is impossible that government should ever degenerate into tyranny." George Washington recognized as much too. In an address to the army, George Washington said, "If men are to be precluded from offering their sentiments on a matter, which may involve the most serious and alarming consequences, that can invite the consideration of mankind; reason is of no use to us—the freedom of speech may be taken away—and, dumb & silent we may be led, like sheep, to the slaughter."[3]

Ultimately, the Founding Fathers knew that America would be on shaky ground if we removed the right of godly citizens to speak the truth. Freedom of speech was a foundational liberty, and if protected it would allow the citizens to protect all other liberties, liberties like the freedom to practice religion. They also knew that if free speech eroded, if people couldn't speak the truth in love, America would slide into chaos and tyranny.

Tyranny of the government?

Tyranny of corporate interests?

Tyranny of the masses?

Yes. Yes. Yes.

Freedom of speech is under attack these days, especially if it's the speech of Christians. Don't believe me? Try speaking about sexuality—or any manner of sin, for that matter—in the public square, the public school, or the public courthouse. If you do, prepare yourself. You'll be called bigoted and hateful. Folks will threaten you with hate-speech legislation. And even if they don't, they'll ridicule you, call you outdated, tell you to shut your trap. Why? It's simple. The American masses killed God, the granter of true liberty, and now they've fallen for this lie of the enemy: freedom of speech shouldn't apply to religious speech, especially when that religious speech touches on issues of sin. Sin speech is called hate speech.

See how it works? Kill'n God ultimately leads to the erosion of God-given liberties.

It doesn't take much to imagine America's slide into tyranny, especially if it's tyranny against Bible-believing folks. But should the day come when the tyranny of the masses takes hold of this country, when the lie of the evil one becomes a legislated prohibition on sharing our faith, what's our responsibility?

- To keep speaking the truth anyway.
- To combat the lies of the enemy with the Word of God.
- To expose sin with our words.
- To tell the world of the coming consequences of that sin.
- To share the rescue that came through Jesus.
- To do all of this, even in the face of persecution like Jesus' early followers did.

Paul lived out this call to speak the truth, even when met with the direst consequences. Enslaved in Rome for preaching the gospel, Paul wrote a letter to the new converts in Ephesus. It read,

Pray also for me, that whenever I speak, words may be given me so that I will fearlessly make known the mystery of the gospel, for which I am an ambassador in chains. Pray that I may declare it fearlessly, as I should. (Eph. 6:19–20)

From that same prison cell, Paul wrote these words to his protégé Timothy:

Remember Jesus Christ, raised from the dead, descended from David. This is my gospel, for which I am suffering even to the point of being chained like a criminal. But God's word is not chained. (2 Tim. 2:8–9)

Behind the bars of tyrannical governments that didn't respect Paul's right to preach the gospel, he was undeterred. Despite lacking free speech, he continued to share the truth.

Why?

Paul understood the plight of men, even of the wicked rulers of the day. He knew they were filled by the evil one, that they needed saving, and he was confident he had the answer. He also knew that folks couldn't respond to the gospel if they didn't hear it first. As he wrote in his letter to the Romans,

How, then, can [sinners] call on the one they have not believed in? And how can they believe in the one of whom they have not heard? And how can they hear without someone preaching to them? (10:14)

Paul knew that the common citizens, the jailers, the rulers of the day—everyone—needed to *hear* the word of truth if they were going to move on it. And so even in prison Paul exercised his God-given freedom to speak, a freedom that couldn't be taken away by anyone.

Even before he was imprisoned Paul knew that preaching the truth would have consequences. He knew he'd be mocked, belittled, beaten, and stoned. Still, he went to the Gentiles and preached the message of the cross. Why? As he wrote to the Corinthian church,

> The message of the cross is foolishness to those who are perishing, but to us who are being saved it is the power of God. For it is written: "I will destroy the wisdom of the wise; the intelligence of the intelligent I will frustrate." . . . For since in the wisdom of God the world through its wisdom did not know him, God was pleased through the foolishness of what was preached to save those who believe. (1 Cor. 1:18–19, 21)

Paul knew the world would find the story of Jesus to be insane. Born of a virgin? Lived a perfect, sinless life? Crucified for our sin? Conquered death on our behalf? Ascended to heaven and is seated at the right hand of the Father? How could a faithless world find that to be anything but foolish? And yet Paul knew it was the kind of foolishness that could save anyone who believed in it.

Children of the Almighty and citizens of America, don't miss this: as people of the narrow road (Jesus' words, not mine), we have an obligation to warn those on the wide road (1 John 5:19). We need to tell those wide-roaders that they're dead in their sins, controlled by the evil one and his minions (Eph. 2:2). And we need to speak this truth in love, in kindness, instructing the wide-roaders in the hopes that God will bring them to repentance (2 Tim. 2:25). See? God told us to speak out—it's our God-given responsibility—so that we might bring freedom to those enslaved to sin.

As for me, I plan to exercise my obligation to speech because I believe the truths of the Bible can save my neighbors from death and my country from chaos. So even if the masses think it's foolishness, even if the government enacts laws to shut me up, I'm gonna keep on preaching. And if the day comes when they tell me I can't call a sin a sin, or I can't spread the good news of Jesus, or I can't talk about how America should return to the truths of the Almighty, guess who they can throw in a jail cell, just like Paul? Me. Why? Because no government will take away my God-given and Founding-Father-recognized right to speak the truth that might save their very souls.

If Jesus is the only hope for an America that's curse'n and kill'n God—and I believe he is—that hope hangs on the Christian's exercise of his or her freedom of speech. Without it, how can we speak truth to the lie?

I've never been one to run from the truth. I've never been one to hold my tongue, either, even when I'm slandered or mocked. Why? Like the Old Testament prophet Jeremiah, the Word of God is shut up in my bones, and I can't hold back (Jer. 20:9). Like the prophet Ezekiel, I understand that if I don't preach the good news of Jesus to those under the control of the evil one, the Almighty will hold me accountable for their death (Ezek. 33:8–9). With so much on the line—the souls of men—how could I hold my tongue? So, what I've received from the Almighty—the Word of Truth—I've preached to the people in hopes they'd find the truth that will save them. I've preached it to river rats and rednecks. I've preached it to prisoners and politicians. I've preached it to celebrities and yuppies. I've even preached it to magazine writers from New York City.

In 2013, at the height of the family's *Duck Dynasty* popularity, I agreed to an interview with one of those city-slicked men's magazines.[4] It was the sort of magazine that features interviews, exercise secrets, and fashion tips. It probably goes without saying, but I ain't one for weightlifting (unless you count lifting a shotgun to my shoulder), and I am not what you'd call a man of high fashion. (Camo pants. A T-shirt. A bandanna. How much more fashionable can you get?) So, it shouldn't have surprised me when the interviewer showed up on the river, wanting to talk about my peculiar way of life, my peculiar family, and my peculiar faith.

We started the day just like any other—a Yamaha, a crossbow, a thermos of coffee, the narrow road—and before long, we were in the thick of nature. As I do with almost everyone who comes to visit, I took him to the fields and showed him the work of the Almighty. I showed him the food supply the Almighty provided for the coming ducks. I showed him the blinds the boys and I had built over the years and gave him a tour of the hunting grounds. I might have shared a few stories with him about beaver trapping and crawfishing, as I'm prone to do. I'm sure I told him about the creativity of our God. I even let him squeeze off a few rounds from my .22—he wasn't a bad shot for a city boy—and let him shoot the crossbow.

When the conversation turned to modern America, I gave it to him straight. We've believed the lies of the Devil, I told him. We've blurred the lines between what's right and wrong and have changed the definition of sin. And so it didn't surprise me a lick when he asked, "What, in your mind, is sinful?" But instead of giving him a piece of my own mind, I gave it to him right out of the Scriptures. He'd later quote me as saying,

> "Start with homosexual behavior, and just morph out from there. Bestiality, sleeping around with this woman and that woman and that woman and those men. . . . Don't be deceived. Neither the adulterers, the idolaters, the male prostitutes, the homosexual offenders, the greedy, the drunkards, the slanderers, the swindlers—they won't inherit the kingdom of God. Don't deceive yourself. It's not right."[5]

Recognize that list? It's the same list laid out right there in Paul's letter to the Corinthians (1 Cor. 6:9–10). It's a recitation of the absolute truth of the Scriptures.

Of course, I didn't stop there. Over the course of the day, I'd preach the full truth of God: there is an eternal penalty for sin, the penalty is eternal death, and the Almighty sent Jesus to conquer death so we could live forever with him. I loved that old boy enough to give him the saving truth, but he didn't move on it, at least not on the spot. And when he'd gathered all the material he needed, he loaded his gear and headed back to his suburban life.

I went about my life and didn't think much more about that interview with the New York City men's magazine—that is, until the magazine published the article and the entire world seemed to lose its collective mind. Gay rights groups said I was homophobic and misinformed. Some accused me of shaming youngsters who were gay. I was called a hate-monger. A number of folks said I shouldn't be allowed one of the most fundamental protections of the United States Constitution—freedom of speech. To add to it, I found myself suspended indefinitely from appearing on *Duck Dynasty*. All this ruckus, and why? Because I'd spoken the truth of the Bible, the truth of the Almighty.

I had plenty of conversations with Miss Kay and my family after that article came out. Miss Kay thought I could have been less blunt. I could have said things with a little more tact. I could have spoken a little less off the cuff. The boys agreed. But not one of them expected me to fall back from the truth of the Bible, and the fact of the matter was, neither did many of the viewers of *Duck Dynasty*. They let the network know they supported me, that they considered me a godly role model for their families. They told the network that my suspension was an attack on my religious views. And so within weeks the network reinstated me. In fact, as it turned out, I didn't miss a single taping of the show.

That turn of events could be a case study on the limits of free speech in modern America. I'd exercised my freedom to speak the truth of God's Word, and those under the influence of the evil one exercised their free speech to influence the television network to suspend me. Many who watched the show, people of faith, used their rights of speech and influenced the network to reinstate me. Speech, speech, speech—we'd all used it for different purposes. And sure, the government didn't step in and keep me from speaking or prosecute me under some hate-speech legislation—an act I think would be in violation of the Constitution—but some suggested they should. Some suggested that creating new legislation might be a way to shut up folks like me in the future.

Enact a law prohibiting me from speaking what the Bible says?

Here in America?

Huh?

In the end everything was sorted out in my favor, and I'm grateful for that. But is it a stretch to imagine a day when the tide turns? Is it hard to imagine a day when the masses, their nonprofits, the worldly corporations, and a corrupt government will work together to shut down the spread of the gospel message? Hardly. There's no better way for a faithless world to insulate itself from conviction and pursue their own desires than to shut down the Christian's right of speech. Just look at Russia, China, and so many of the Muslim-controlled countries. See how quickly tyranny can spread when the evil one persuades us with his lies, primarily the lie that Christians shouldn't have the right to speak the truth?

The Bible teaches me to love my neighbor as much as I love myself, and I love myself enough to try and avoid the eternal punishment for all my sins. So if I'm to love my neighbor just as much, shouldn't I do whatever I can to warn my brothers of the coming punishment for their sin? Shouldn't I exercise my freedom of speech to that end?

No doubt.

It's not hate speech to give someone the truth that will save their souls. It's love speech. And so no amount of public ridicule from faithless people, no godless group, and no number of high-minded professors can keep me from sharing the truth in love. A magazine article poking fun at me won't keep me from sharing the truth in love. Losing sponsors or sales or money won't stop me from sharing the truth in love. And if the government enacts tyrannical laws that keep me from sharing my faith, that won't keep me from speaking the truth in love either. Why? I have an obligation to share the truth that sets men free.

Regardless of the consequences.

Regardless of whether the world thinks it's foolishness.

After all, it's that foolishness that might save their souls.

Interview after interview, time after time, the media has attacked my love for Jesus and my commitment to his truth. As we say down here in Louisiana, it don't bother me a lick. Jesus used his freedom to preach the truth all the way to the cross. Paul used his freedom of speech to preach the good news even when it landed him in prison and cost him his life. God's people are his prophetic voice in America, and it's time to use our freedom to preach the good news. If we do, we can turn this ship around before we lose our right to speak.

THE TRUTH OF TRUTHS

Little by little, lie by lie, the lines of morality, decency, and virtue have moved in America. I can still remember the America of 1966, the year *Time* asked the infamous question, "Is God Dead?" If you'd told me then how different America would look fifty years later, I wouldn't have believed you. I couldn't have fathomed America's abortion epidemic, wouldn't have thought I'd live in a country where hundreds of thousands of babies are aborted every year. Even though I wasn't really the praying kind, I wouldn't have believed prayer would be pushed out of school. I'd never have imagined so much chaos, so many violent protests or mass shootings. And if you'd told me that in fifty years marriage would no longer be defined as being between a man and a woman, I'd have called you insane.

As I've written in these pages, the enemy of America's soul has come to steal, kill, and destroy. He's slicked us, convinced us generation by generation to take one step further away from the absolute truth of God. How's he done it? He's sold us these ten lies: (1) God is dead; (2) there is no Devil; (3) truth is relative; (4) God did not create life; (5) sex is for self-gratification; (6) virtue is outdated; (7) laws can be ignored or changed if they are inconvenient; (8) unity is not possible; (9) church participation and day-to-day life should be kept separate; and (10) Christians should shut their traps.

But as I showed in this book, we can return to God if we recognize those lies and live into these truths of the Almighty: (1) the God of the Bible is not dead and he never will be; (2) the Devil of the Bible is real and he is our enemy; (3) there is absolute truth and it comes from God; (4) God is the Author of life and he wants to fulfill it; (5) God created sexuality for his purposes and our good; (6) God's standard for all time is the standard of virtue; (7) law and order come from the Word of God; (8) unity flows from a God-centered culture; (9) the church is God's presence in the day-to-day world, keeping the world from becoming hell on earth; and (10) God's people are his prophetic voice in the world. These truths aren't just powerful in word. As I hope you've seen throughout this book, if we stay true to them, they'll set people free.

This, I suppose, brings me to the ultimate truth, the truth from which all the other truths of this book flow. The Almighty loves you, me, and the rest of America. He loves us so much, he sent Jesus to earth to teach us that perfect truth, to live a sinless life, and to conquer sin and death. What's more, he clearly communicated the story of Jesus through the Scriptures. From Genesis to Malachi, the Almighty told us to pay attention because Jesus—the Savior of the world—was coming. From Matthew to John, the writers told us to pay attention because Christ had come. In Acts through Revelation, the writers reminded us that Christ is coming again, and when he comes, he'll honor those who've honored him and punish those who've fallen for the evil one's lies.

What'll happen to those children of the enemy? It'll be the eternal lake of fire for those dudes. I wouldn't wish that on anyone. Especially my friends here in America.

What should we do with this great truth of truths, the truth of the Almighty's love? We should put our faith in it and organize our whole lives around it. As Paul wrote to the Ephesians, we should "follow God's example, therefore, as dearly loved children and walk in the way of love, just as Christ loved us and gave himself up for us as a fragrant offering and sacrifice to God" (5:1–2). But merely believing the truth isn't enough. We also stake our lives on it. We preach, preach, preach, in duck season and out of duck season (my paraphrase of 2 Timothy 4:2). Every day. All day. Unapologetically. We must preach the news of God's love in our public schools, our public squares, and our voting booths. We speak of the Almighty's saving power—to the teachers and principals, the mayors and governors, or in my case, President Trump himself. We remind the world that Jesus has made a way for them to conquer misery, disease, and death. In eternity? Yes. But here too.

Why do we preach the truth so relentlessly? Because we love our neighbors as much as we love ourselves.

I suppose some who are under the delusions of the evil one will read this book, challenge my love for them, and maybe even accuse me of hate speech for calling out their sin. I suspect they'll call me a crazy old graybeard for preaching the truth in these pages the only way I know how. They can say whatever they like, because the truth is, I've given my life to this message, and I only know one way to preach it—*with great zeal*. "Zeal?" you ask. That's right. Zeal. That's how Paul taught us to preach when he wrote to the Romans, "Never be lacking in zeal, but keep your spiritual fervor, serving the Lord" (12:11). What is zeal? *Merriam-Webster* defines it as "intense heat." It's the boiling point. So when folks see my passion for the things of God, when they call me a Bible banger or a zealot, when they mock me for preaching the good news, they're simply recognizing the heat. That ain't a bad thing.

I've adopted an open-carry policy when it comes to my zeal for God. It's that open-carry policy that's made me a target in the media, this much is true. They've held my faith under the microscope of public scrutiny, but they haven't caught me in any scandal. They haven't caught me drinking or doing drugs or running around on Miss Kay. Instead, they've only found one thing—an unwavering commitment to the absolute truth of who Jesus is and how his love can change a life. It's this unwavering commitment that's led folks like Big Al Bolen, or that gentleman from Minnesota, or the old boy living with his girlfriend, or the countless prisoners at Angola, or the woman in the rehab, or the fella from Decatur, or the hundreds of others who've visited my homestead on the river to accept the saving message of Jesus. It's this unwavering commitment that's led many down into the waters of baptism.

I first learned that kind of zeal, that unwavering commitment to the truth of the Almighty's love, from my sister, Jan.

Before my life with Christ, my running buddies and I had a saying posed in the form of a question: "Who's a man?" It was a question we'd ask before a good party, a hard fight, or an evening of whoring around. We were convinced that real men did what they wanted, that they chased down and fulfilled every desire. We'd bought the lie of the evil one—*there is no moral authority; desires are made to be chased; freedom means doing whatever we want.* Buying into that lie, we'd become lawless rednecks. We were rough, tough, and sometimes violent. We ran hard as the Devil, convinced we had no need for the Almighty. In fact, Jesus himself might have been speaking about the boys and me when he said,

"You belong to your father, the devil, and you want to carry out your father's desires. He was a murderer from the beginning, not holding to the truth, for there is no truth in him. When he lies, he speaks his native language, for he is a liar and the father of lies." (John 8:44)

Son of the Devil as I was, I didn't care a lick about changing my ways, and I wasn't ashamed to say as much. If you'd have known me back in those days, you'd have said I'd be the last person to darken the doors of a church. I was a lost cause, too far gone. Why wasn't I interested in changing my ways even though I felt so empty? Why wasn't I interested in reforming even after I lost my teaching job in Junction City, even after I lost my bar and trailer, even in the days just after Miss Kay left? For starters I had no idea what it really meant to be free. I'd never been told the good news about Jesus, the news that would set me free from the lies of the enemy and the misery those lies brought. I'd never been told I could escape sin, shame, and the grave. I had no idea I could have eternal health care, free of charge. But add to that the fact that I watched folks going in and coming out of their Sunday morning church services, and for the most part, they didn't seem all that different from me. Many of them frequented my bar. Some of them ran around the woods with me. And the rest of the Christians I knew didn't seem to be happy, happy, happy. To put it plainly, Christians didn't seem to be all that much like Christ.

But unruly as I was, violent as I was, whoremonger that I was, my sister, Jan, never gave up on me. Sure, she believed in me, but more importantly, she believed the power of God could free me. Jan knew the truth: God wasn't dead. In fact, he was quite alive and he had the power to rescue me from the chaos of my life. She knew how to put feet to her faith too. And so she dragged the preacher-man Bill Smith into the darkest place to reach me—a backwoods beer joint.

Years after my baptism, Jan told me how much she believed in the power of God's love to change my life. She told me what she'd said to Bill before they walked into that bar to share the gospel with me. "Bill," she said, "if you lead Phil to Jesus, he'll bring thousands along with him." What did she see in me? I'll never know. But I know this much: everyone needs a sister who believes in the truth of God as much as Jan.

Turns out Jan was right. Eventually, after my life fell apart, after I found myself hollowed out and imprisoned by my own desires, after Bill Smith led me into the waters of baptism, I discovered the power of Jesus' words: "Then you will know the truth, and the truth will set you free" (John 8:32). I've experienced the true freedom that comes when we turn our backs on the lies of the evil one and walk in the power of the Almighty—freedom from sin, from guilt, from a law of works I could never keep, from the grave itself. That's why I share the saving message of Jesus with everyone I come across. That's why I tell them how it will set them free if only they'll trust it. And though I haven't kept a strict count of the number of folks who've come to Jesus through my message, I reckon Jan was right. Hundreds, if not thousands, have come to faith because I've shared this message. And it all started with Jan.

My story isn't a testament to me. It's a testament to the saving power of a living and loving God. It's the story of how the truth of Jesus can change one man, how it can spread through one man to feed thousands—friends, business acquaintances, customers, and television viewers alike. My story is just one example of how the truth of the gospel can change the masses, truth by truth, person by person. And if enough of us begin to live into this transformative truth of God's love, if we combat the lies of the enemy with the truth of Scriptures, if we preach the truth in the darkest places—just like Jan and Bill did—what might happen here in America? My guess is we'd see God's saving power take hold of this country. We'd see people turn back to God. If enough folks turned and gave their lives to the Almighty, I believe we'd see a country committed to God once again. We'd find ourselves with virtuous leaders, leaders courageous enough to enact godly laws and stand against evils like abortion and the changing definitions of marriage. We'd return to civility, to the brotherly love that trumps division and hate. Through the power of the Almighty, we'd become a more unified people.

So here's my parting shot, America. Pay attention to the marching orders Jesus left us:

> "Therefore go and make disciples of all nations, baptizing them
> in the name of the Father and of the Son and of the Holy Spirit,
> and teaching them to obey everything I have commanded you.
> And surely I am with you always, to the very end of the age."
> (Matt. 28:19–20)

Rest assured: until I take my last breath, I aim to carry out these orders. Join me in the mission of proclaiming the truth of God's love to an America who's been sold a bill of goods, a country who is intent on kill'n God. And as you go into the darkest places to preach that truth, know this: Jesus is with you as you go, all the way to the end.

ACKNOWLEDGMENTS

Thanks to Seth Haines, Sealy Yates and his team, the Nelson Books team, Kairos Group, Zack Dasher, Ben Adkins, and Al Robertson.

ABOUT THE AUTHOR

PHIL ROBERTSON, the founder and co-owner of the Duck Commander Company, is a professional hunter, successful businessman, and the popular star of A&E's reality television series *Duck Dynasty*. He is also the host of the new subscription television series *In the Woods with Phil* on CRTV.com. He authored two *New York Times* bestselling books, *Happy, Happy, Happy* and *UnPHILtered*. He and his wife, Kay, live in West Monroe, Louisiana. Together, they have four grown sons and daughters-in-law, sixteen grandchildren, and seven great-grandchildren.

NOTES

INTRODUCTION

1. John T. Elson, "Toward a Hidden God," *Time*, April 8, 1966.
2. Frank Newport, "Most Americans Still Believe in God," Gallup, June 29, 2016, https://news.gallup.com/poll/193271 /americans-believe-god,aspx.

CHAPTER 2

1. Sabrina Tavernise, "U.S. Suicide Rate Surges to a 30-Year High," *New York Times*, April 22, 2016, https://www.nytimes.com/2016/04/22 /health/us-suicide-rate-surges-to-a-30-year-high.html.
2. "Marriage and Divorce," American Psychological Association, http ://www.apa.org/topics/divorce/.
3. "CDC's Abortion Surveillance System FAQ," Centers for Disease Control and Prevention, last updated https://www.cdc.gov /reproductivehealth/data_stats/abortion.htm.

CHAPTER 3

1. John T. Elson, "Toward a Hidden God," *Time*, April 8, 1966.

CHAPTER 4

1. "Scopes Trial," Wikipedia, https://en.wikipedia.org/wiki/Scopes_Trial.
2. Steven Ertelt, "60,069,971 Abortions in America Since Roe v. Wade in 1973," LifeNews.com, January 18, 2018, http://www.lifenews.com/2018/01/18/60069971-abortions-in-america-since-roe-v-wade-in-1973/.

CHAPTER 5

1. CDC Fact Sheet, Reported STDs in the United States, 2017, https://www.cdc.gov/nchhstp/newsroom/docs/factsheets/std-trends-508.pdf.
2. CDC Fact Sheet, Reported STDs.
3. Abby Goodnough, "Reported Cases of Sexually Transmitted Diseases Are on Rise," *New York Times*, October 19, 2016, https://www.nytimes.com/2016/10/20/us/reported-cases-of-sexually-transmitted-diseases-are-on-rise.html.
4. CDC Fact Sheet, Reported STDs.

CHAPTER 6

1. Independence Hall Association, "In His Own Words," *The Autobiography of Benjamin Franklin*, http://www.ushistory.org/franklin/autobiography/page38.html.
2. "In His Own Words," *The Autobiography of Benjamin Franklin*.
3. "Farewell Address," The Papers of George Washington, http://gwpapers.virginia.edu/documents_gw/farewell/transcript.html.
4. "John Adams Diary 1, 18 November 1755–29 August 1756," *Adams Family Papers: An Electronic Archive*, Massachusetts Historical Society, https://www.masshist.org/digitaladams/archive/.

CHAPTER 7

1. John Adams to Thomas Jefferson (June 28, 1813), as quoted by Michael Novak in "Meacham Nods," *National Review*, December 13, 2007, https://www.nationalreview.com/2007/12/meacham-nods-michael-novak/.
2. Patrick Henry to Archibald Blair (January 8, 1799), Patrick Henry Memorial Foundation Digital Library, http://patrickhenrylibrary.org/islandora/object/islandora%3A1075.

3. Last Will and Testament (20 November 1798), as quoted in *Patrick Henry: Life, Correspondences and Speeches* (1891) by William Wirt Henry, vol. H, 631.

4. As quoted by Hon. Jack Kingston of Georgia, Thursday, June 27, 2002, United States of America Congressional Record, *Proceedings and Debates of the 107th Congress*, 2nd ed., vol. 148, pt. 9, June 27 to July 15, 2002, 12403.

5. John Quincy Adams, *An Oration Delivered Before the Inhabitants of Newburyport*, (Massachusetts: n.p., 1837), 6.

6. John Quincy Adams, *Letters of John Quincy Adams to His Son on the Bible and Its Teachings* (Auburn, NY: Derby, Miller & Co., 1848), 61.

7. Quoted in Horace W. Fuller, ed., *The Green Bag*, vol. 2 (Boston: The Boston Book Company, 1891), 264.

8. Quoted in Daniel L. Dreisbach, *Reading the Bible with the Founding Fathers* (New York: Oxford University Press, 2017), 45.

9. William W. Story, ed., *Life and Letters of Joseph Story*, vol. 1 (Boston: Charles C. Little and James Brown, 1851), 92.

10. United States Supreme Court Decision in Church of the Holy Trinity v. United States, 143 U.S. 457 (1892), Justia, https://supreme.justia.com/cases/federal/us/143/457/case.html.

11. "Address before the Attorney General's Conference on Law Enforcement Problems," Harry S. Truman Presidential Library and Museum, https://www.trumanlibrary.org/publicpapers/index.php?pid=657.

12. Gerhard Peters and John T. Woolley, "Ronald Reagan: Proclamation 5018—Year of the Bible, 1983," February 3, 1983, The American Presidency Project, http://www.presidency.ucsb.edu/ws/?pid=40728.

CHAPTER 9

1. Emma Green, "It's Hard to Go to Church," *The Atlantic*, August 23, 2016, https://www.theatlantic.com/politics/archive/2016/08/religious-participation-survey/496940/.

2. Anugrah Kumar, "Are Most Single Christians in America Having Sex?," *Christian Post*, September 28, 2011, https://www.christianpost.com/news/are-most-single-christians-in-america-having-sex-56680/.

3. Guttmacher Institute, "Induced Abortion in the United States,"

January 2018, https://www.guttmacher.org/fact-sheet
/induced-abortion-united-states.

4. Meredith Somers, "More Than Half of Christian Men Admit to
Watching Pornography," Washington Times, August 24, 2014,
https://www.washingtontimes.com/news/2014/aug/24
/more-than-half-of-christian-men-admit-to-watching-/.

CHAPTER 10

1. Thomas Jefferson, "Notes on the State of Virginia,
Query XVIII: Manners," Teaching American History,
http://teachingamericanhistory.org/library/document
/notes-on-the-state-of-virginia-query-xviii-manners/.

2. Benjamin Franklin, "Silence Dogood, No. 8," printed in *New-England
Courant*, July 9, 1722, National Archives Founders Online, https
://founders.archives.gov/documents/Franklin/01-01-02-0015.

3. "George Washington to the Officers of the Army," March 15, 1784,
National Archives Founders Online, https://founders.archives.gov
/documents/Washington/99-01-02-10840.

4. Drew Magary, "What the Duck?" *GQ*, December 17, 2013, https
://www.gq.com/story/duck-dynasty-phil-robertson?currentPage=2.

5. Drew Magary, "What the Duck?"